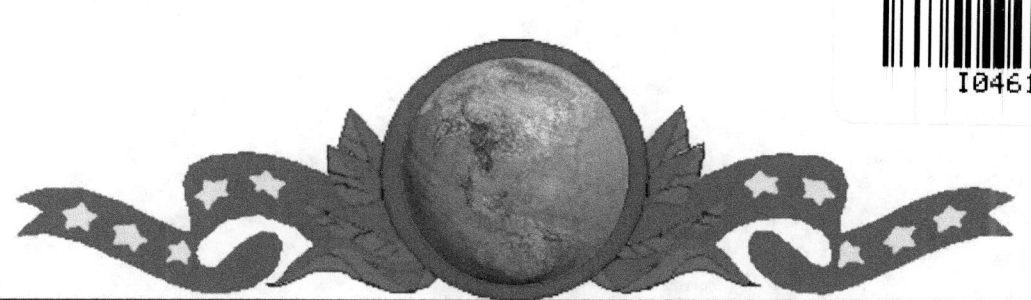

# Real World
## *Colouring Book*
### For Advanced Users & Adults

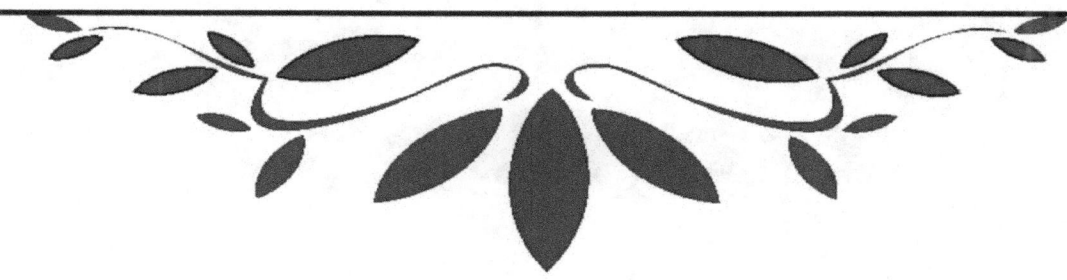

Copyright 2019 By John Boom

## 50 Images

## Created From Real Life Photos
## For You To Colour As You Please.

ISBN 978-0-359-83501-0

90000

9 780359 835010

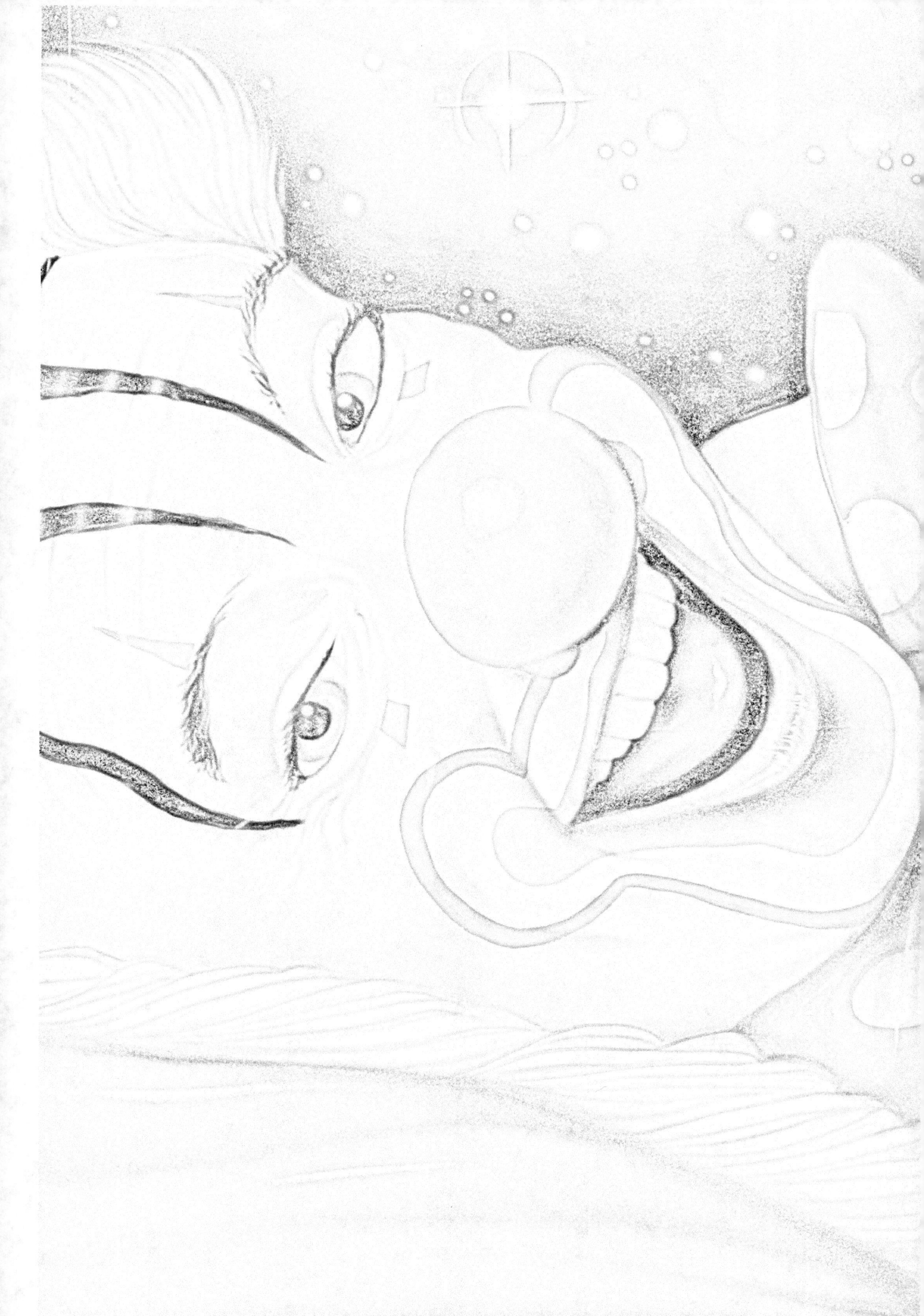

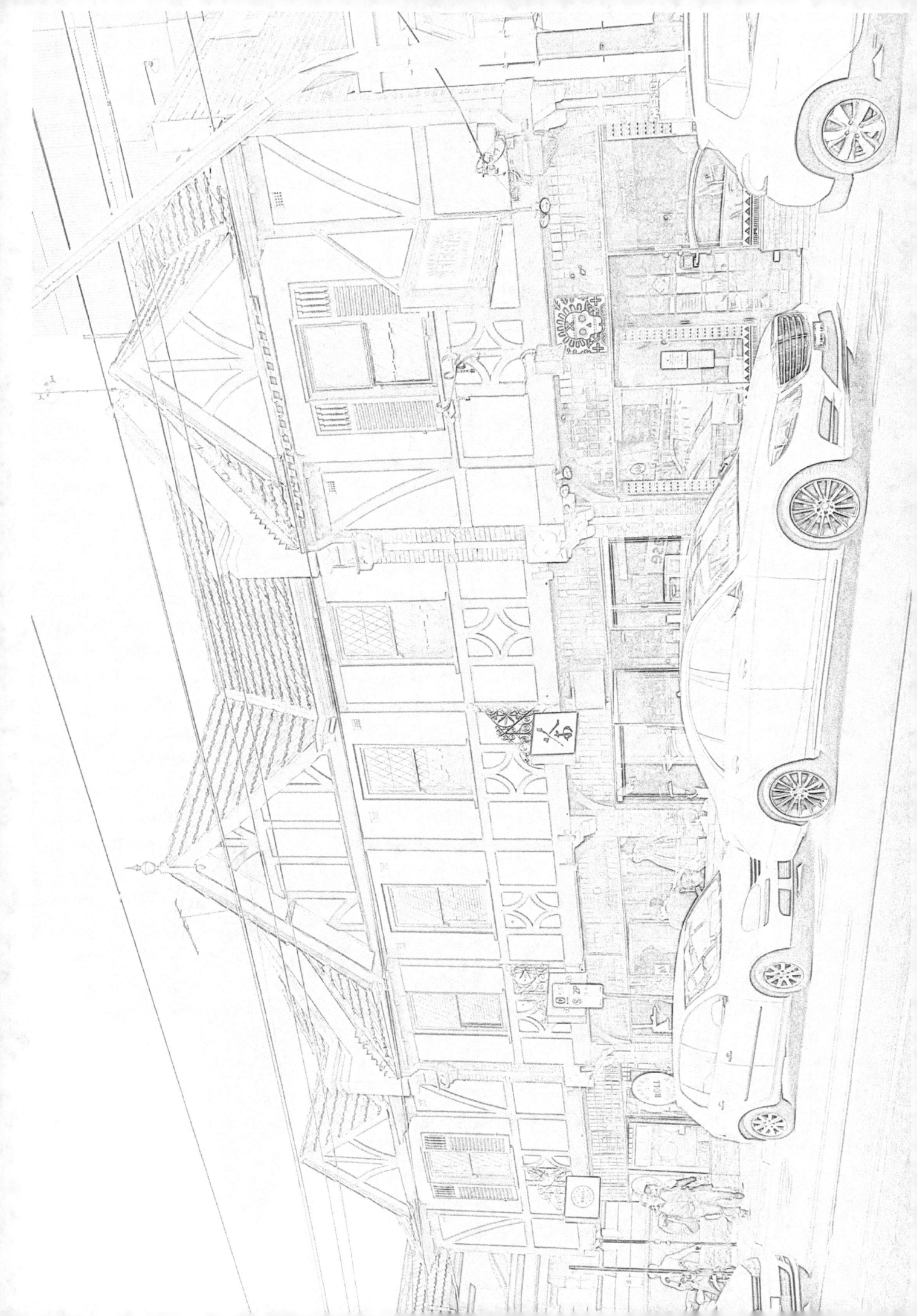

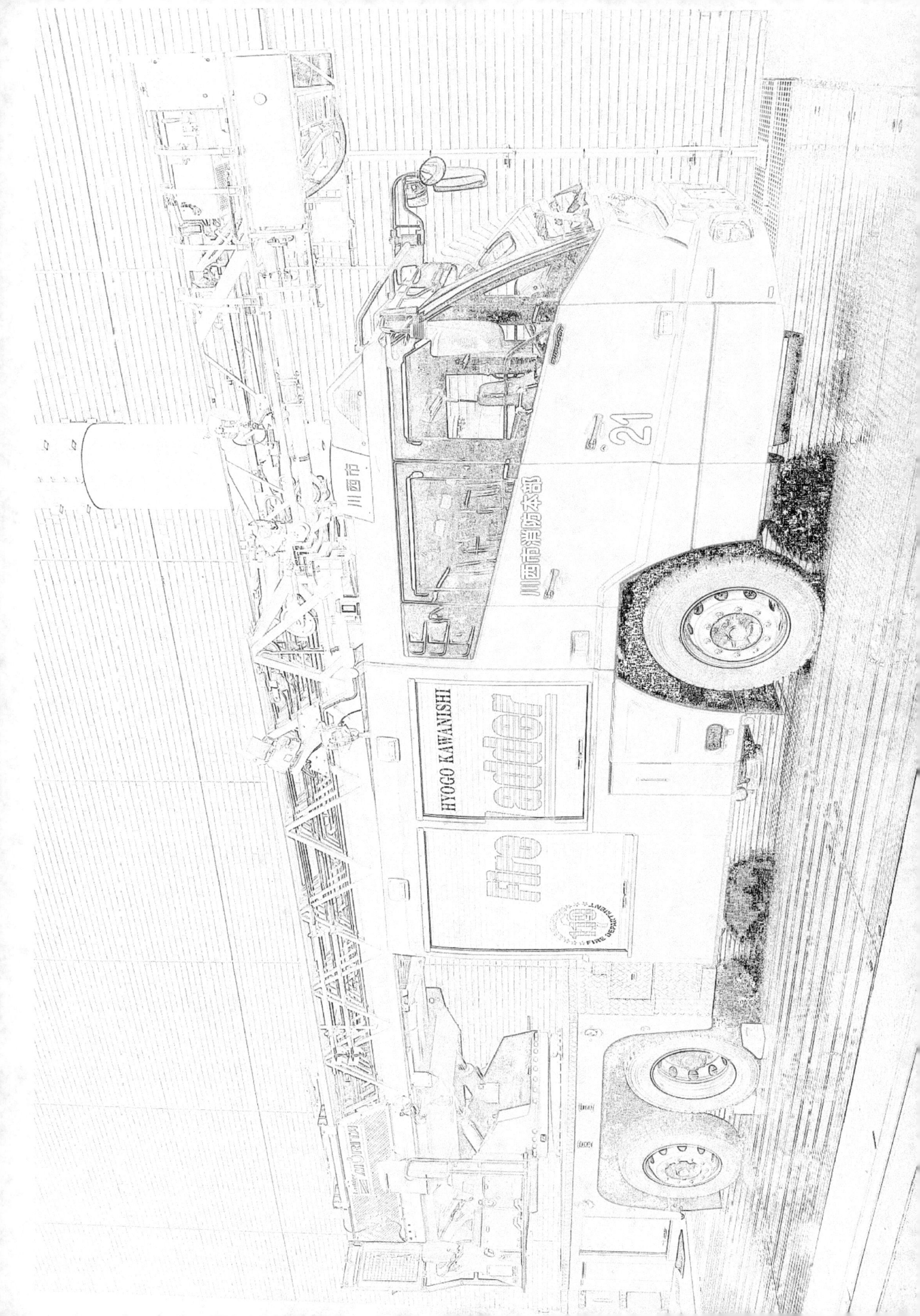

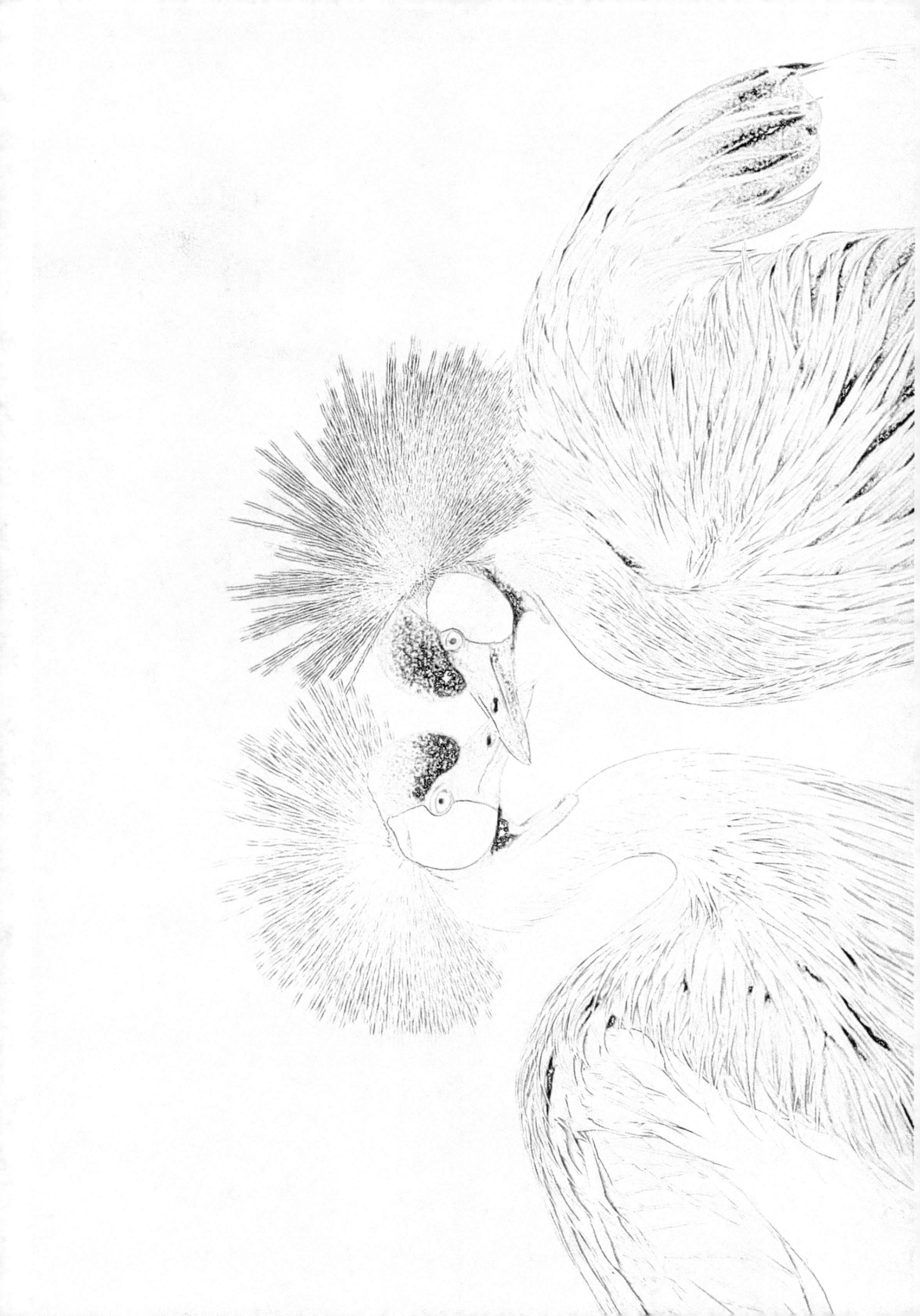

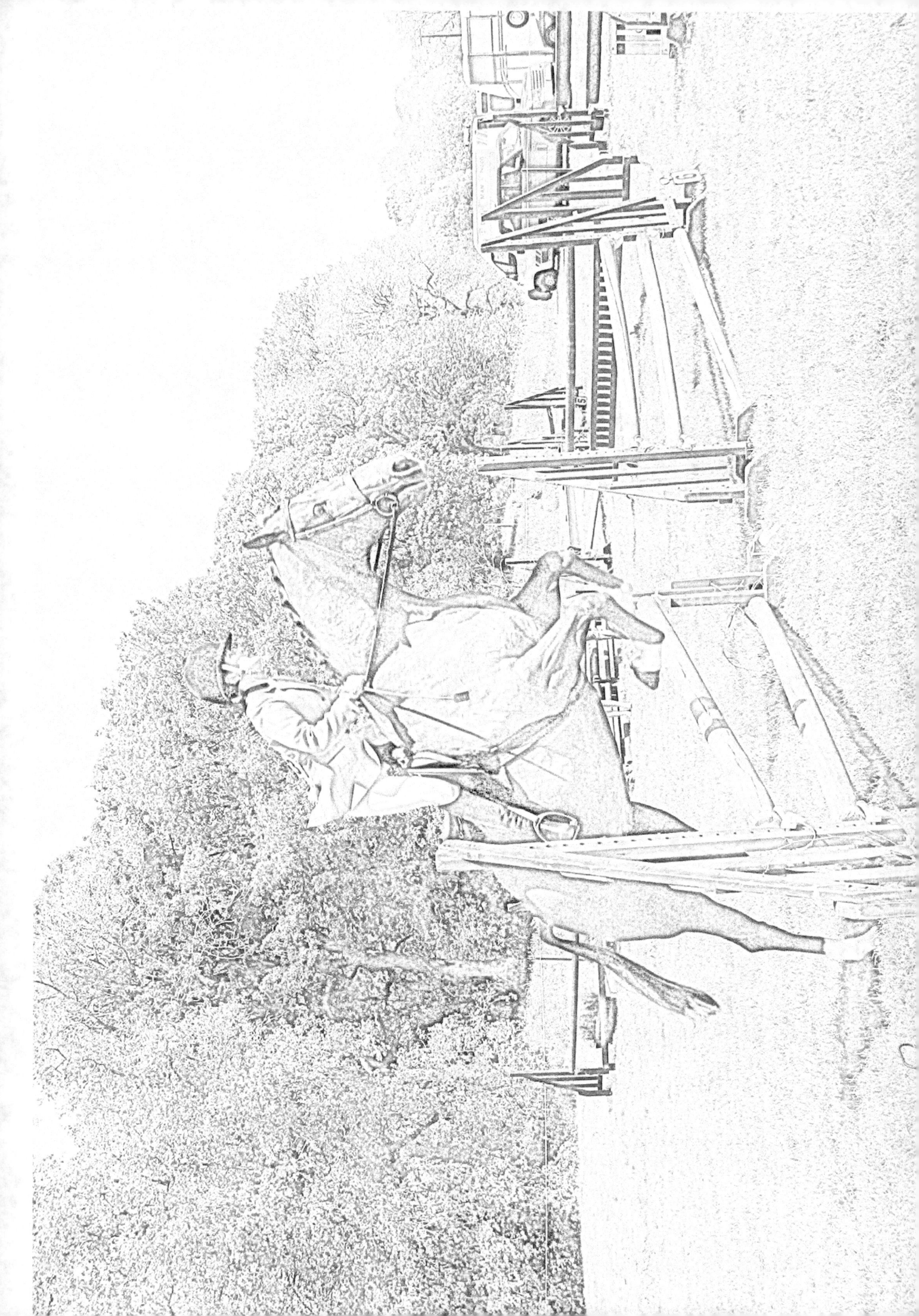

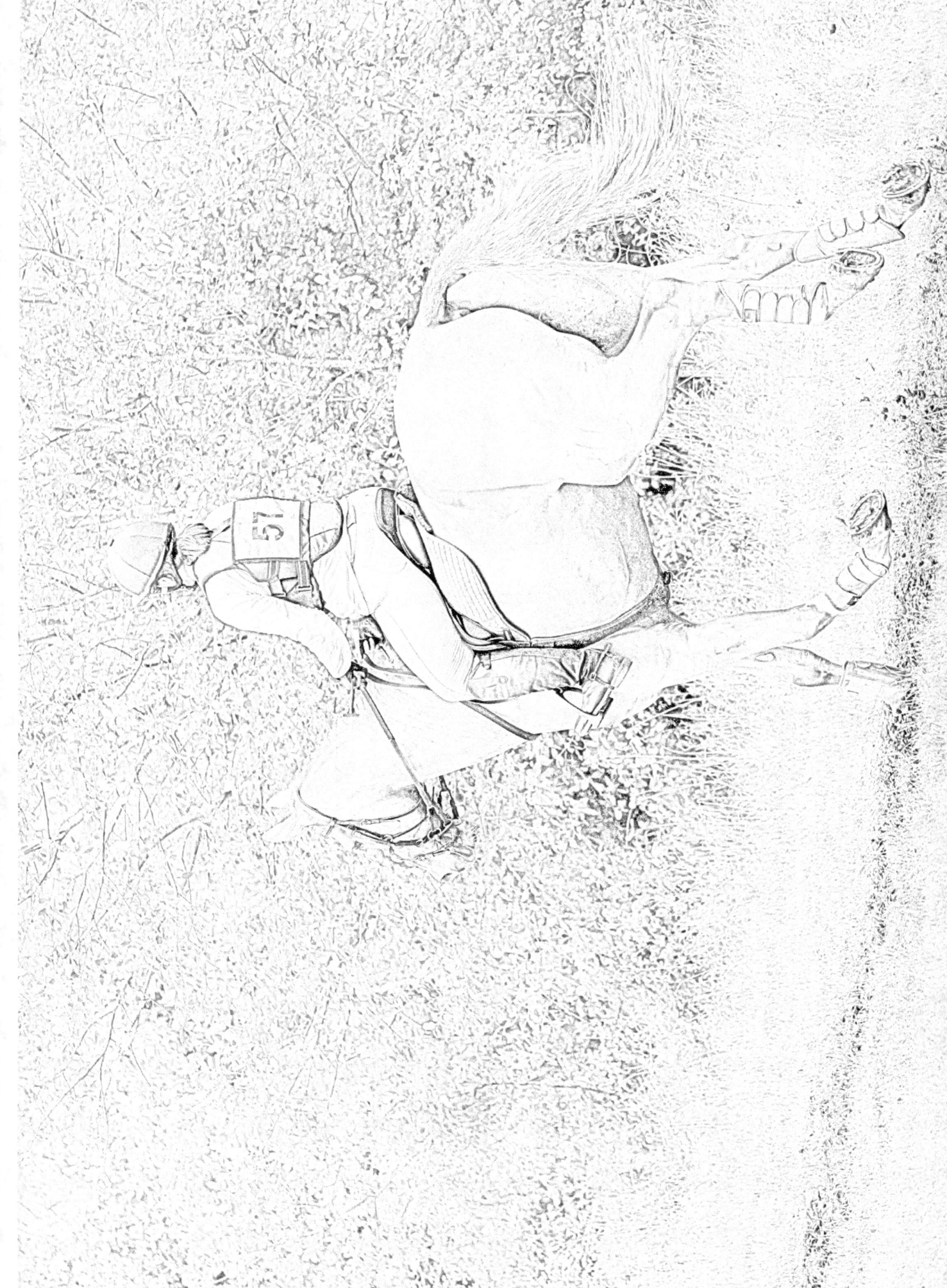

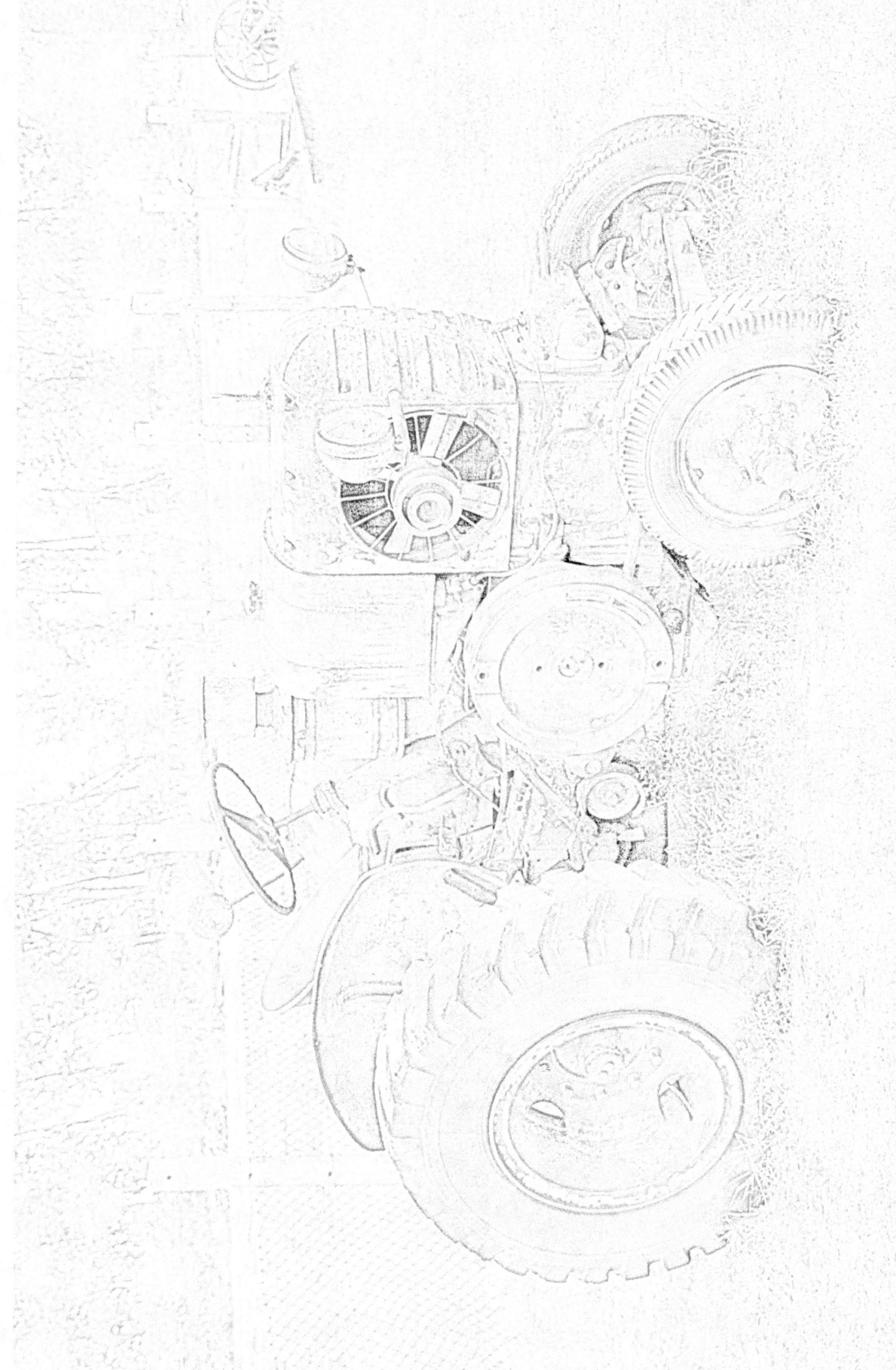

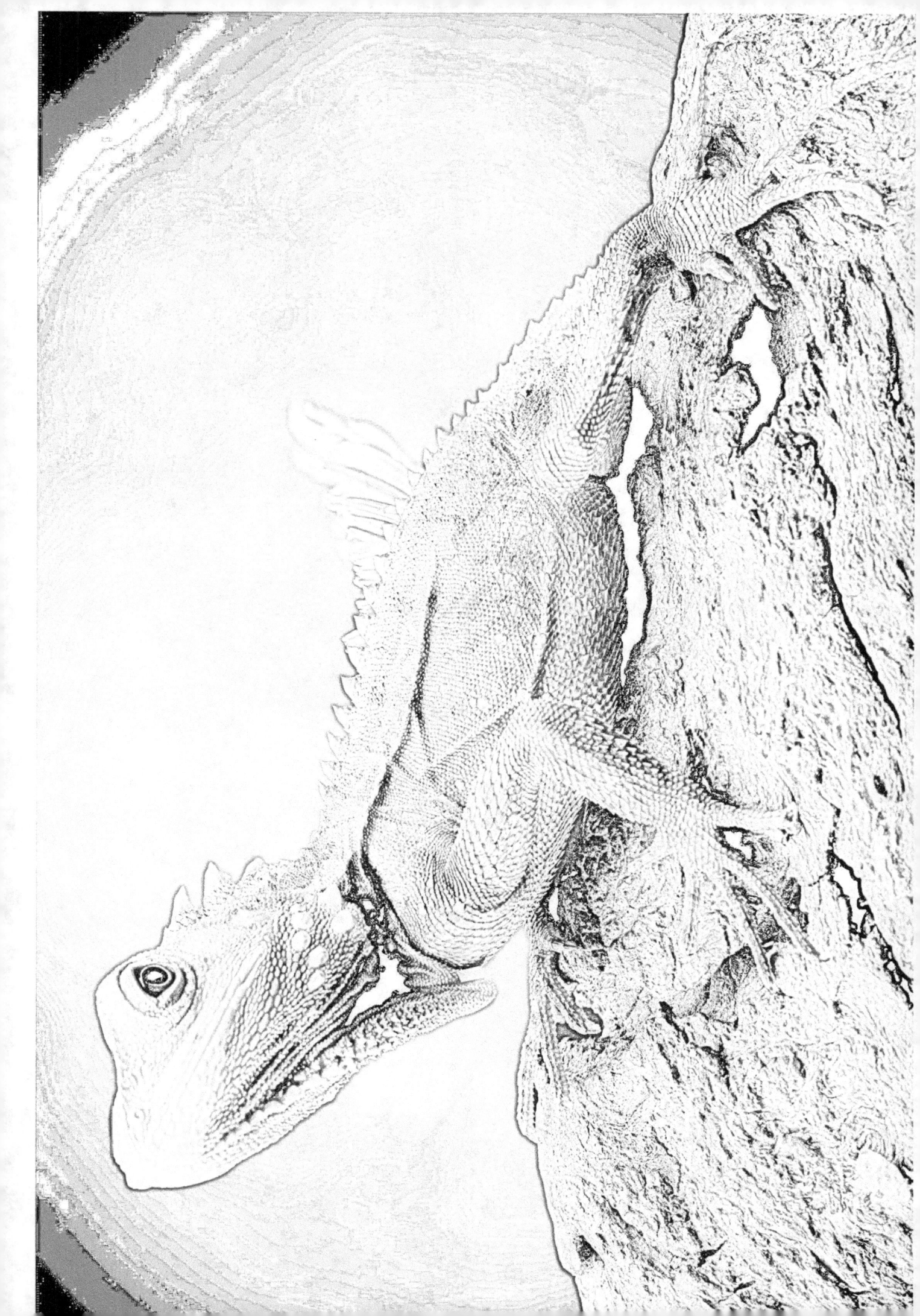

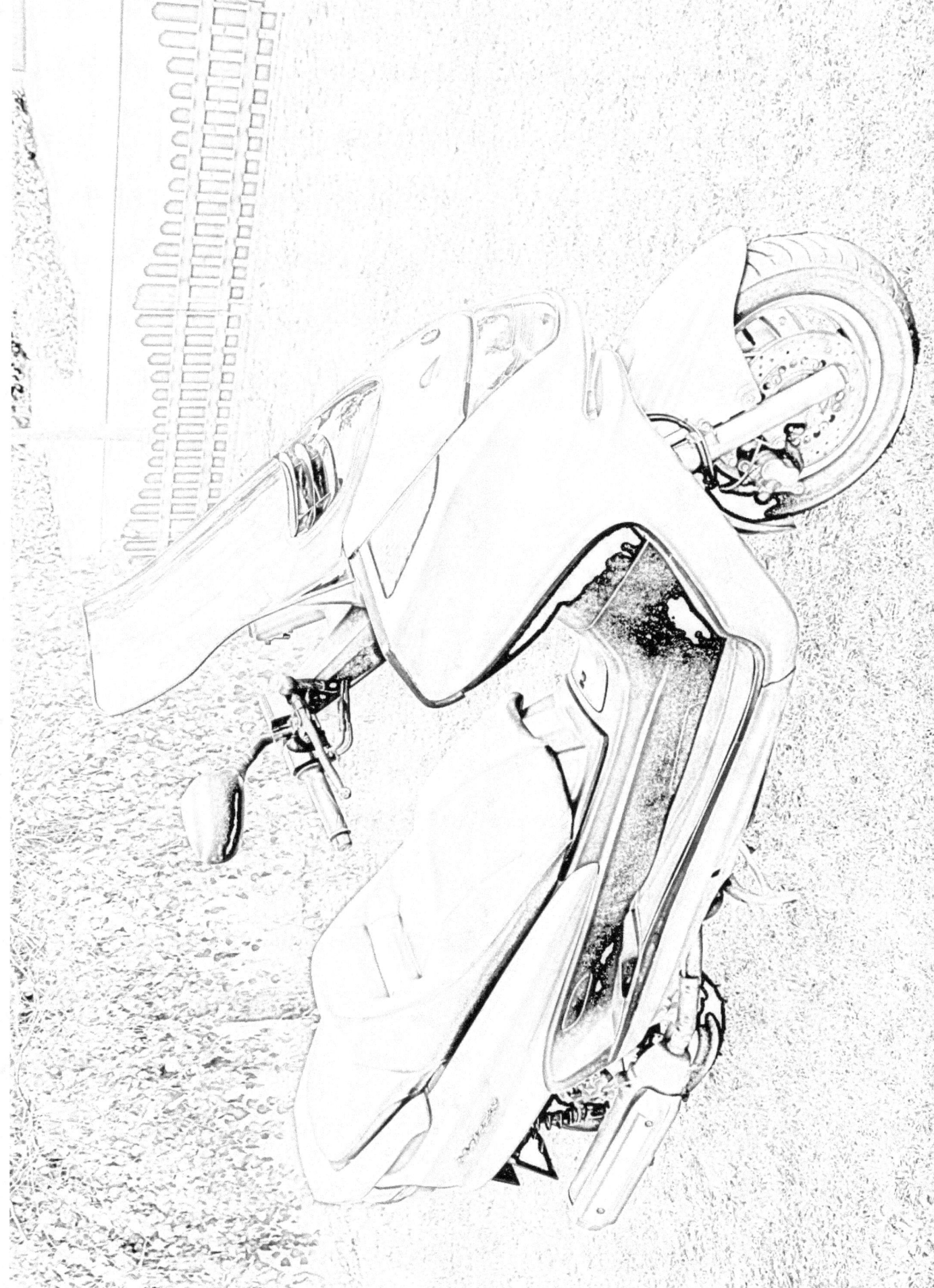

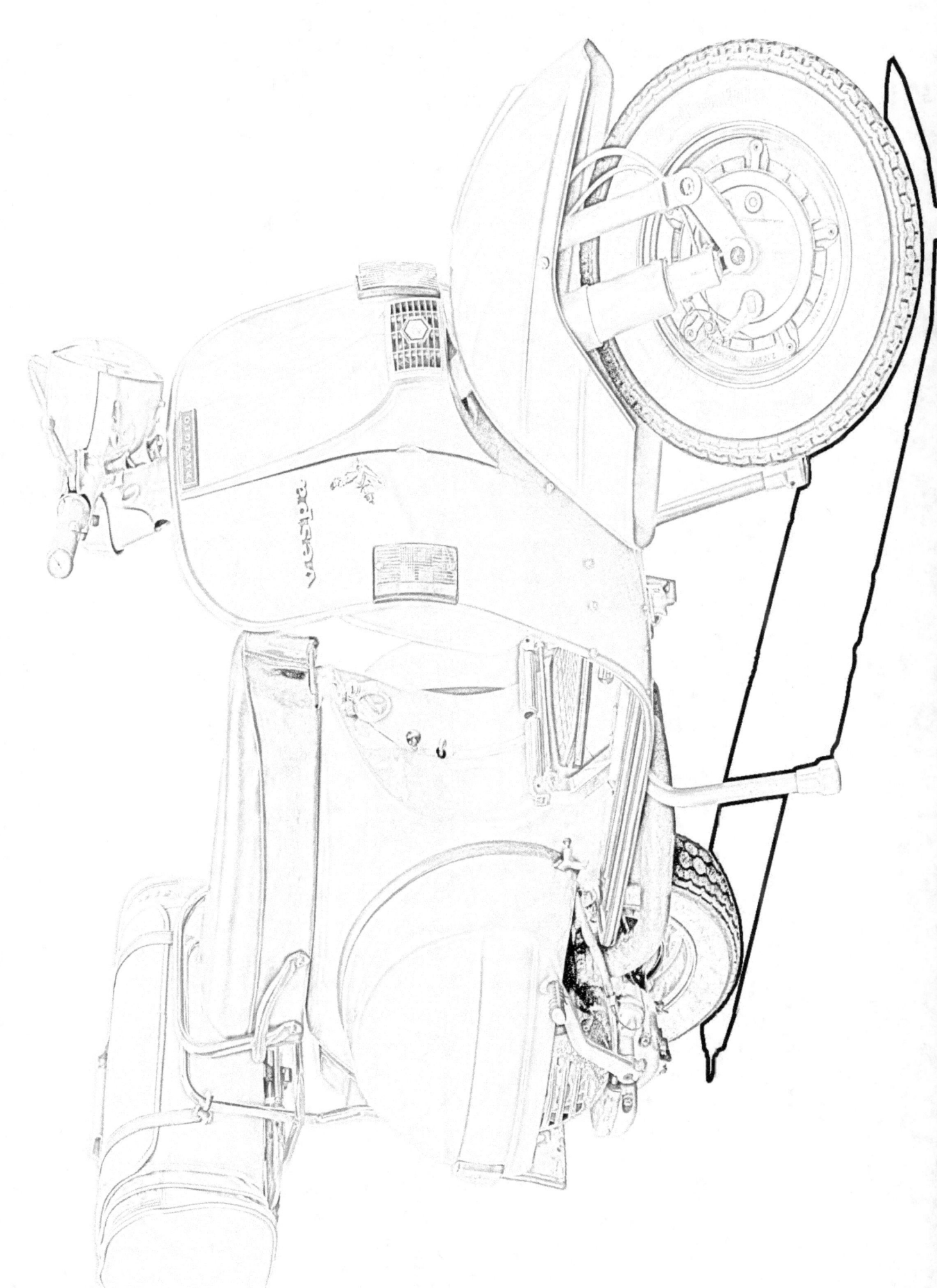

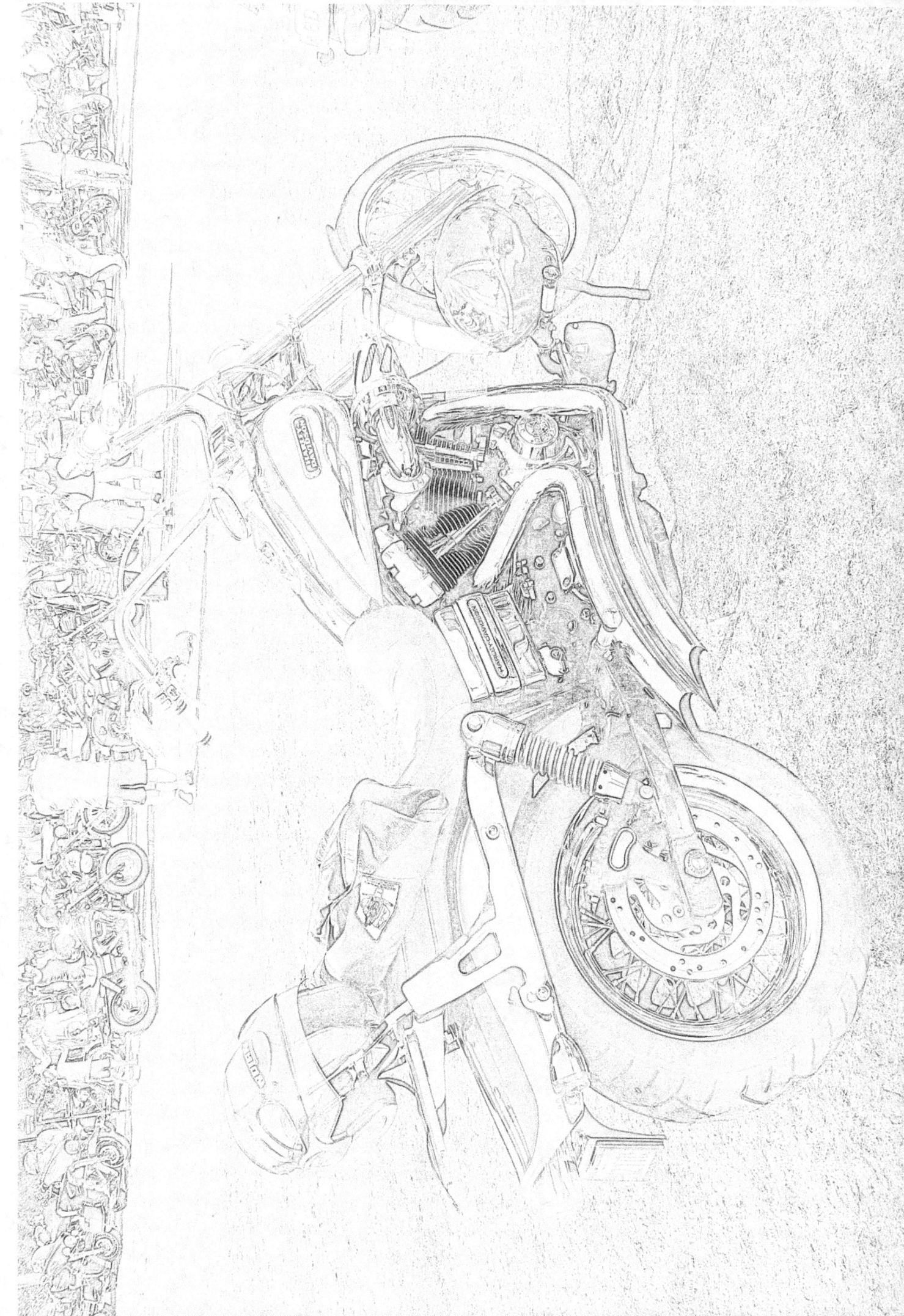

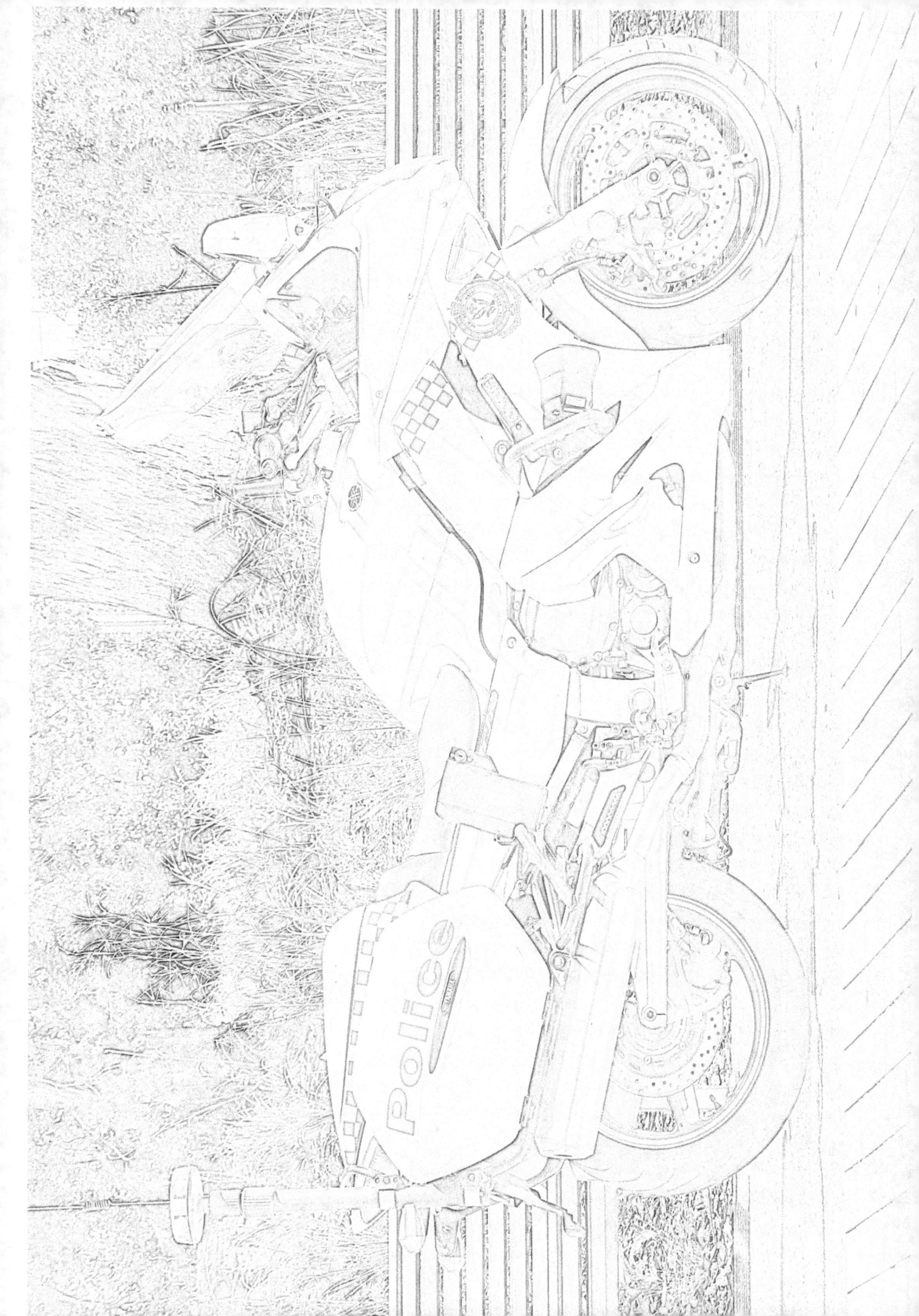

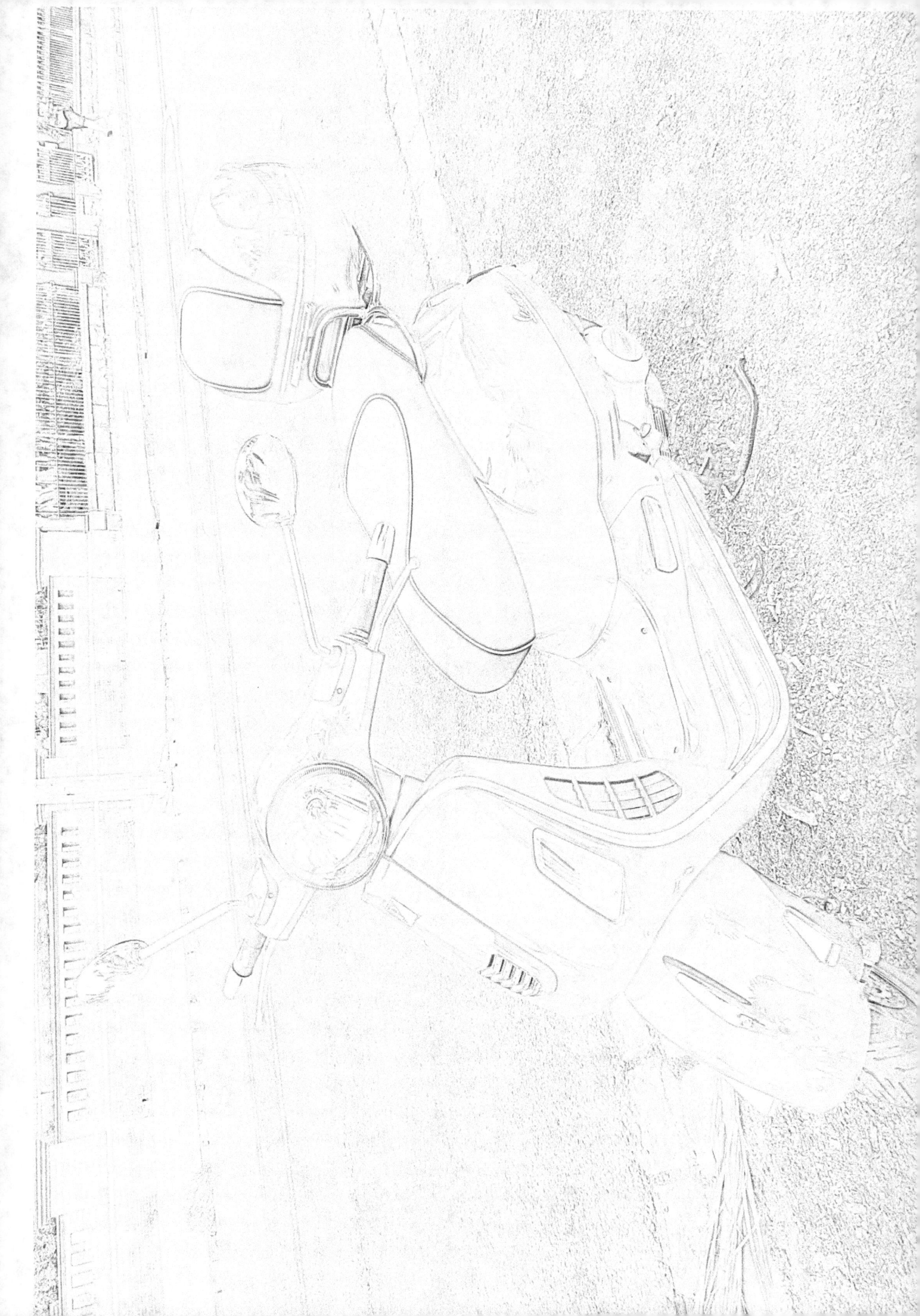

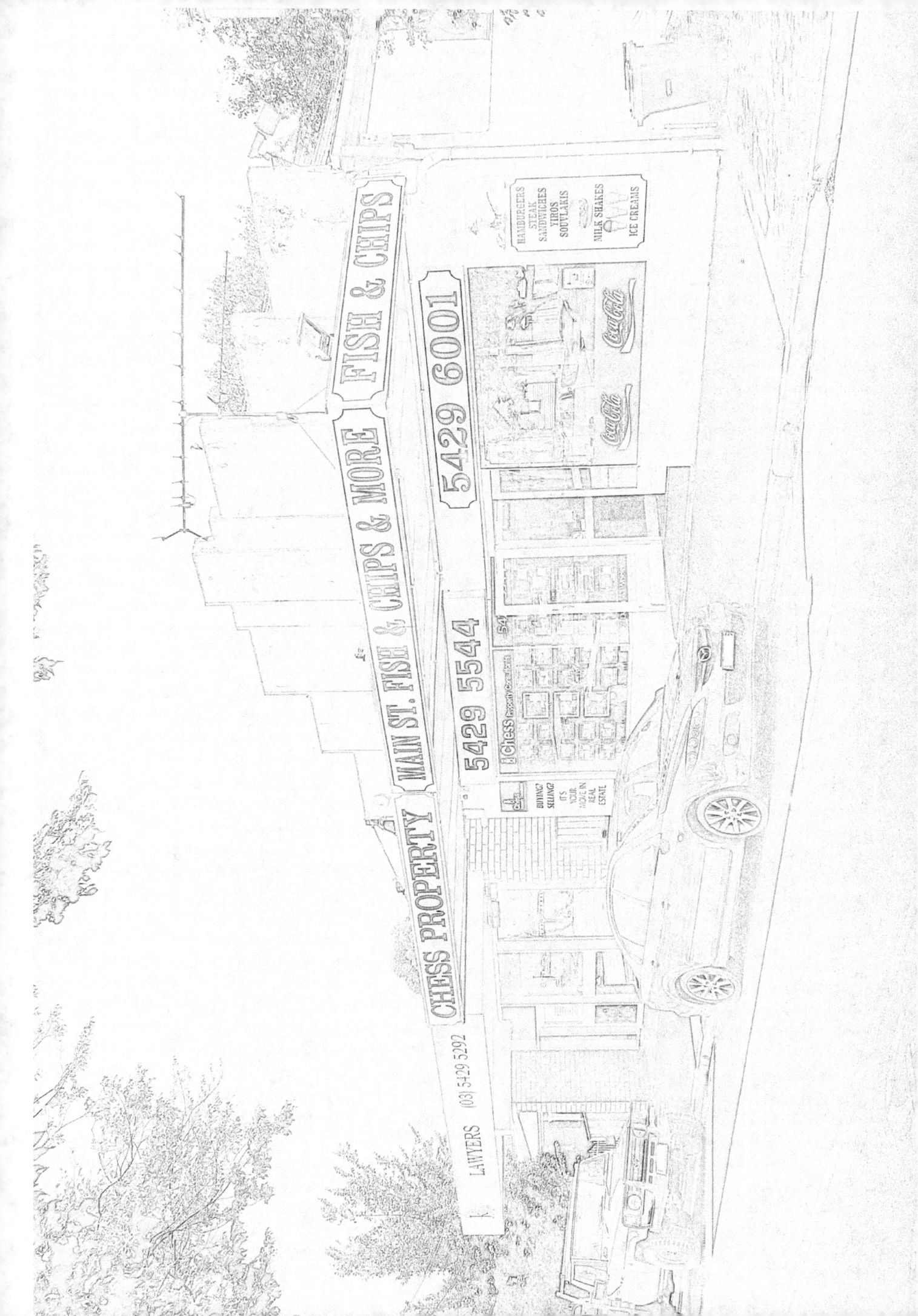

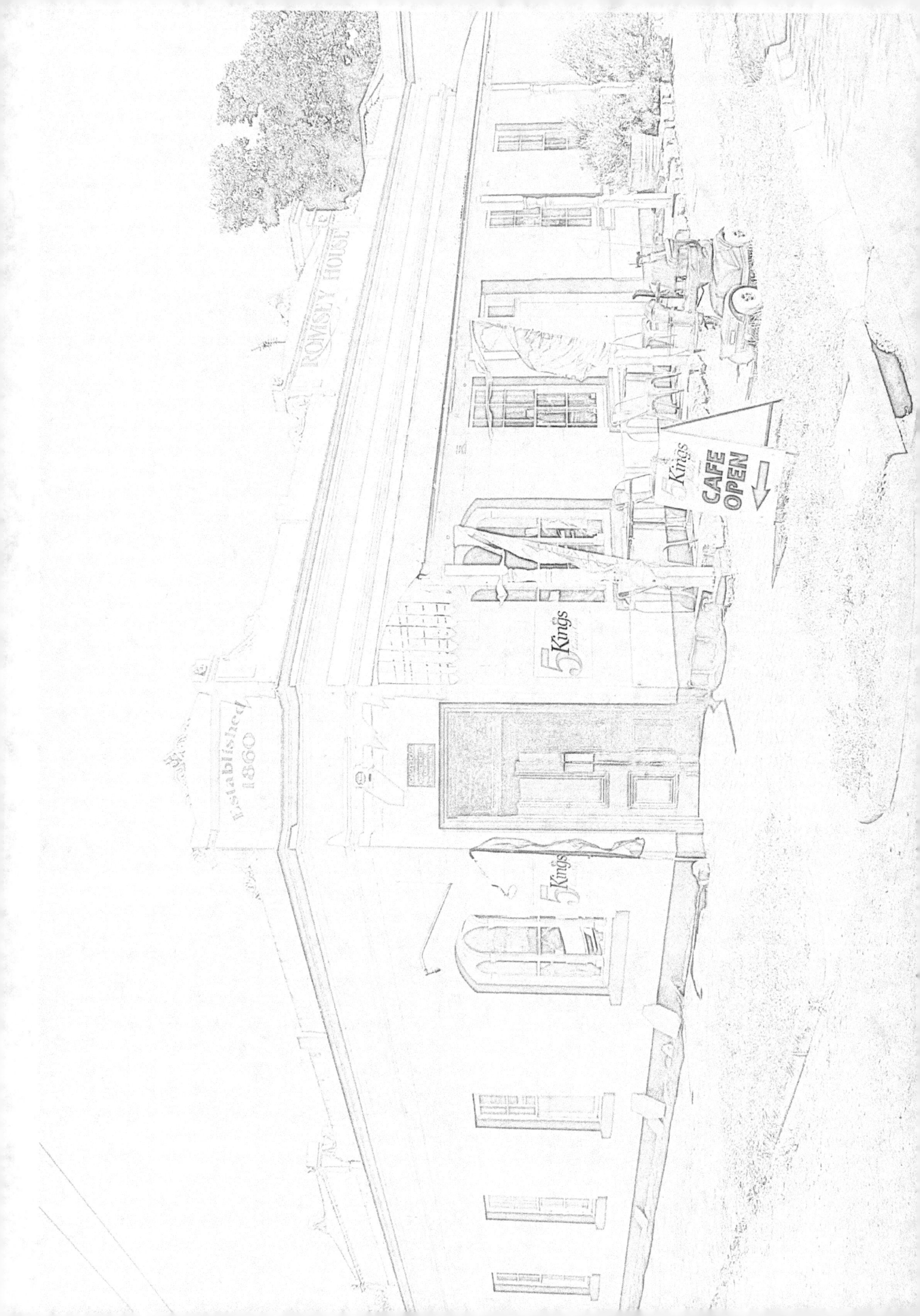

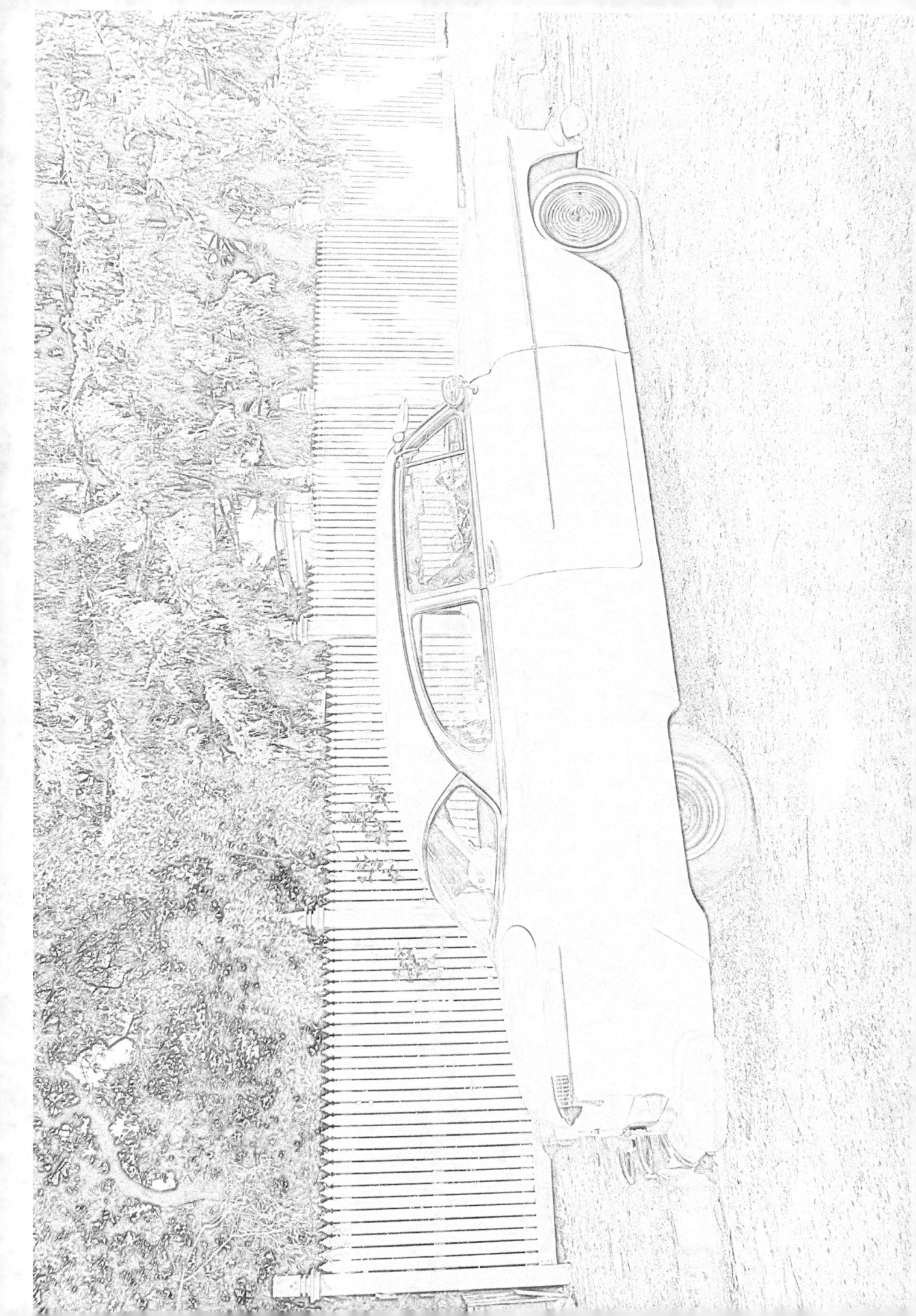

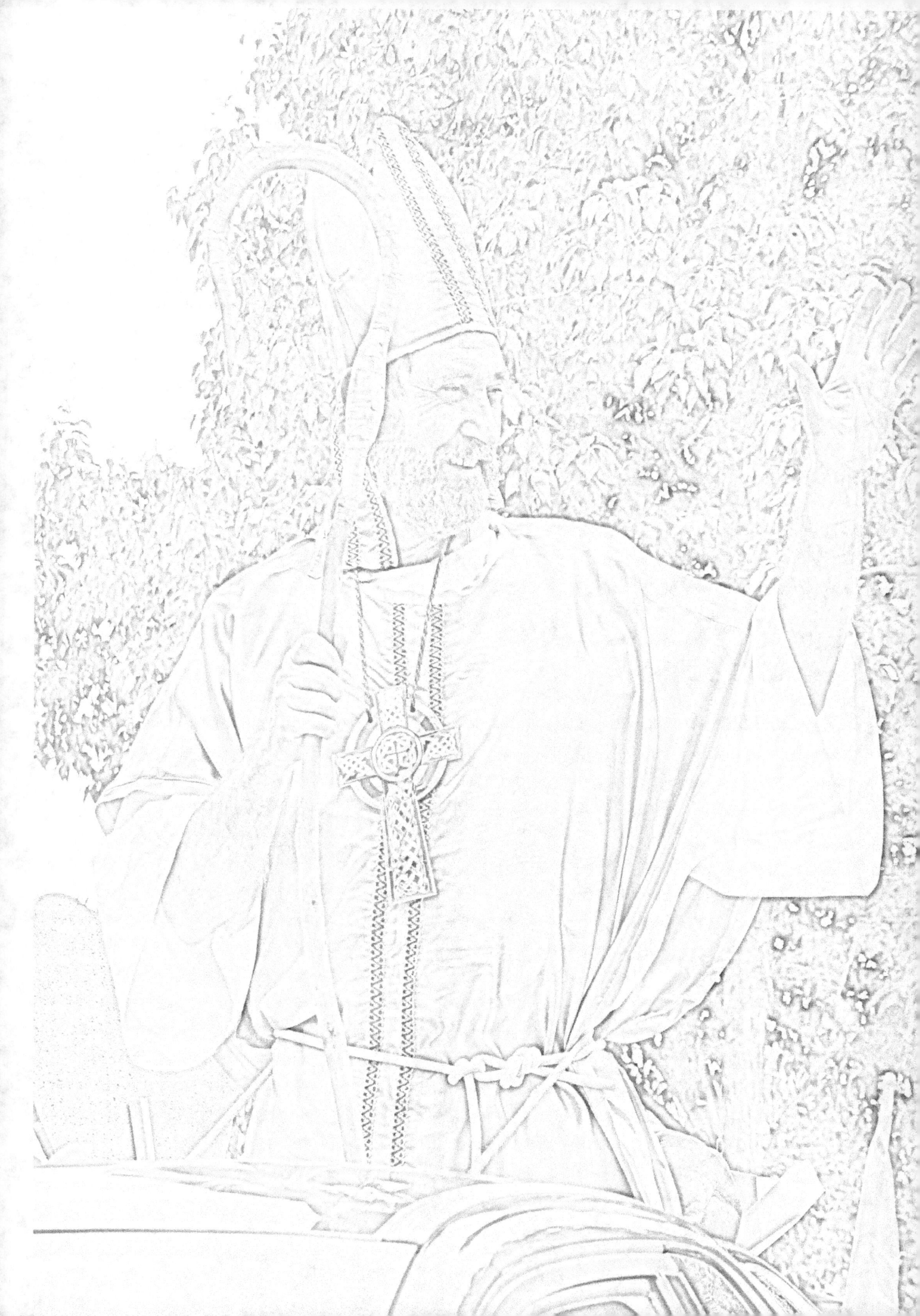

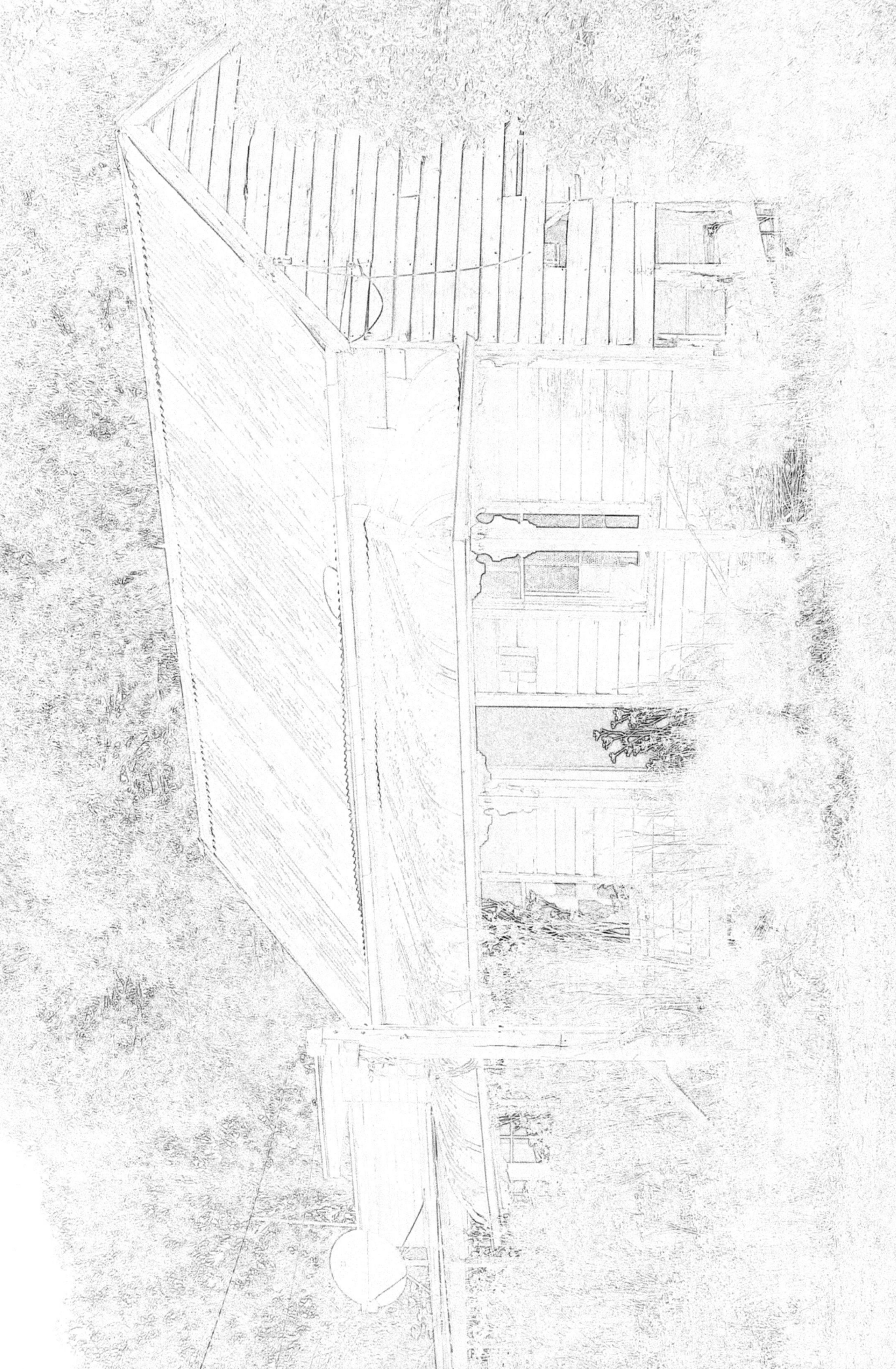

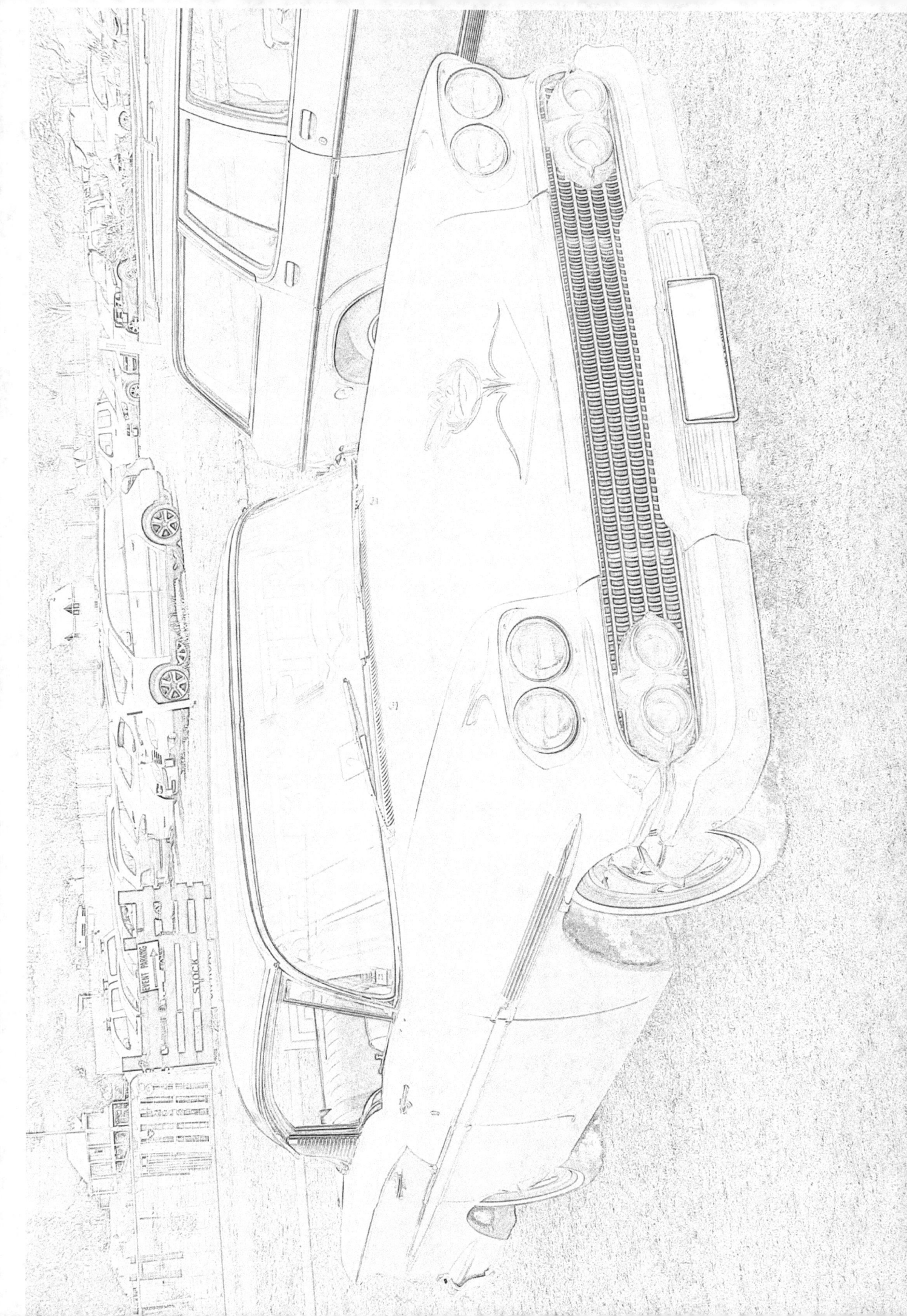

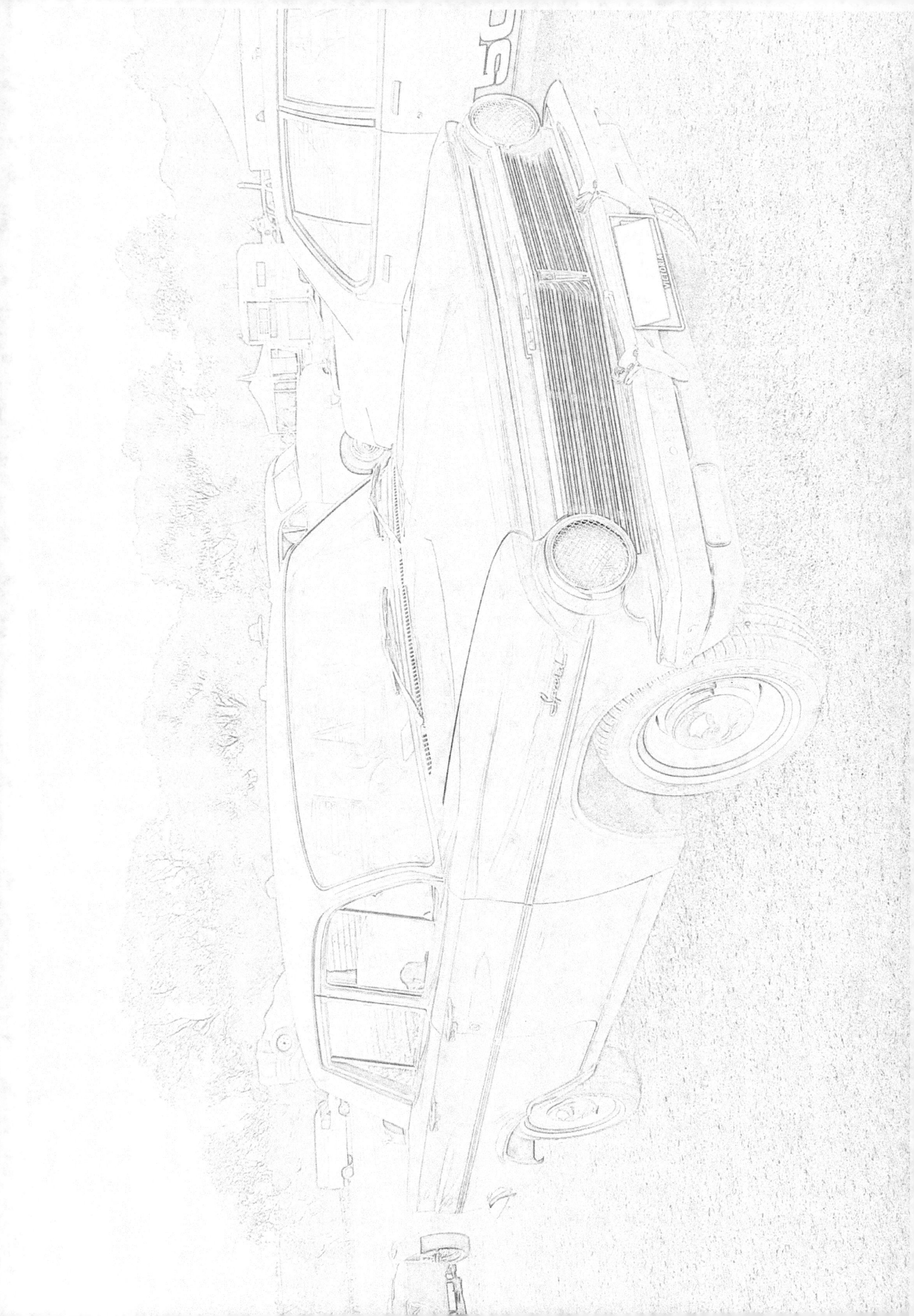

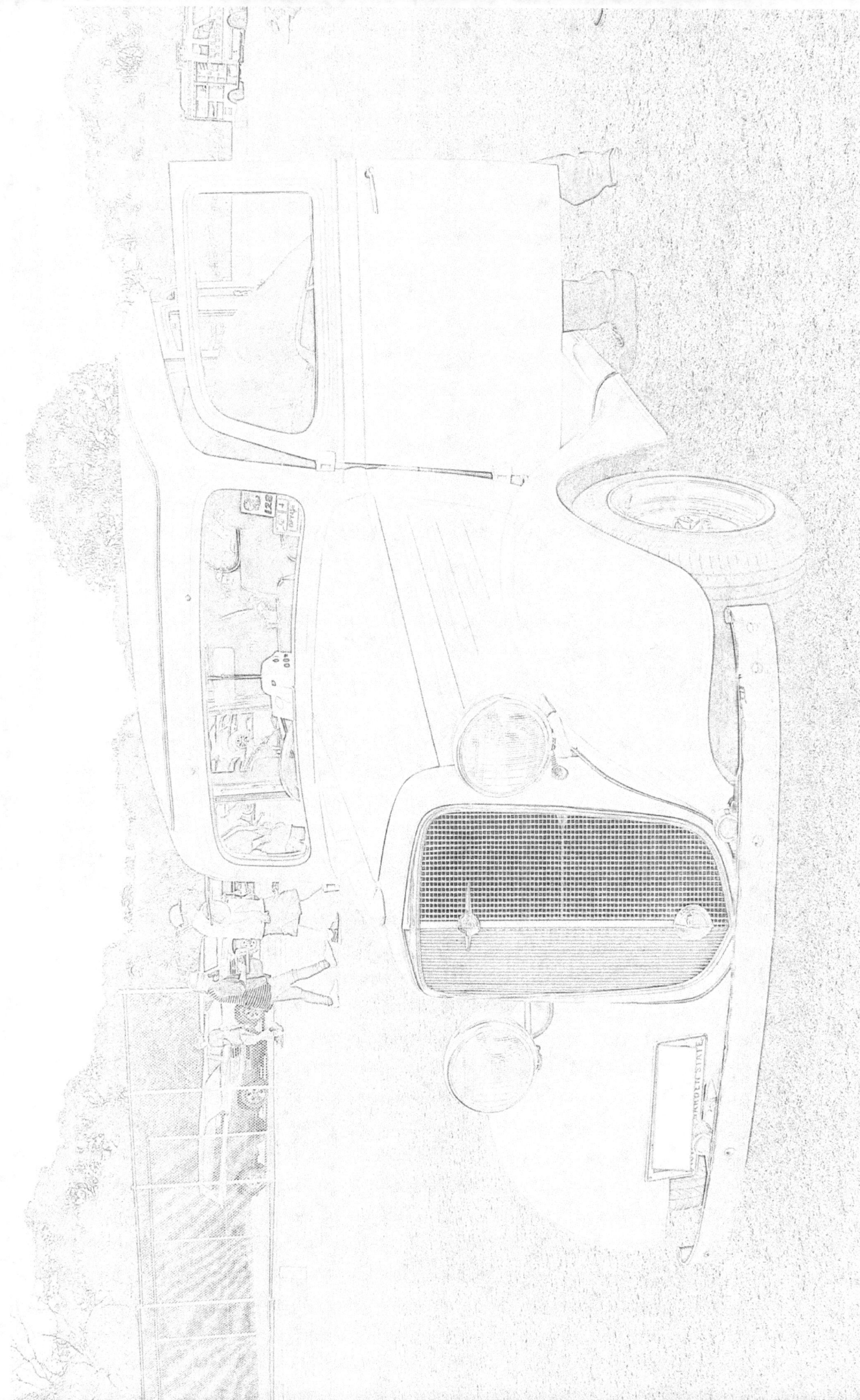

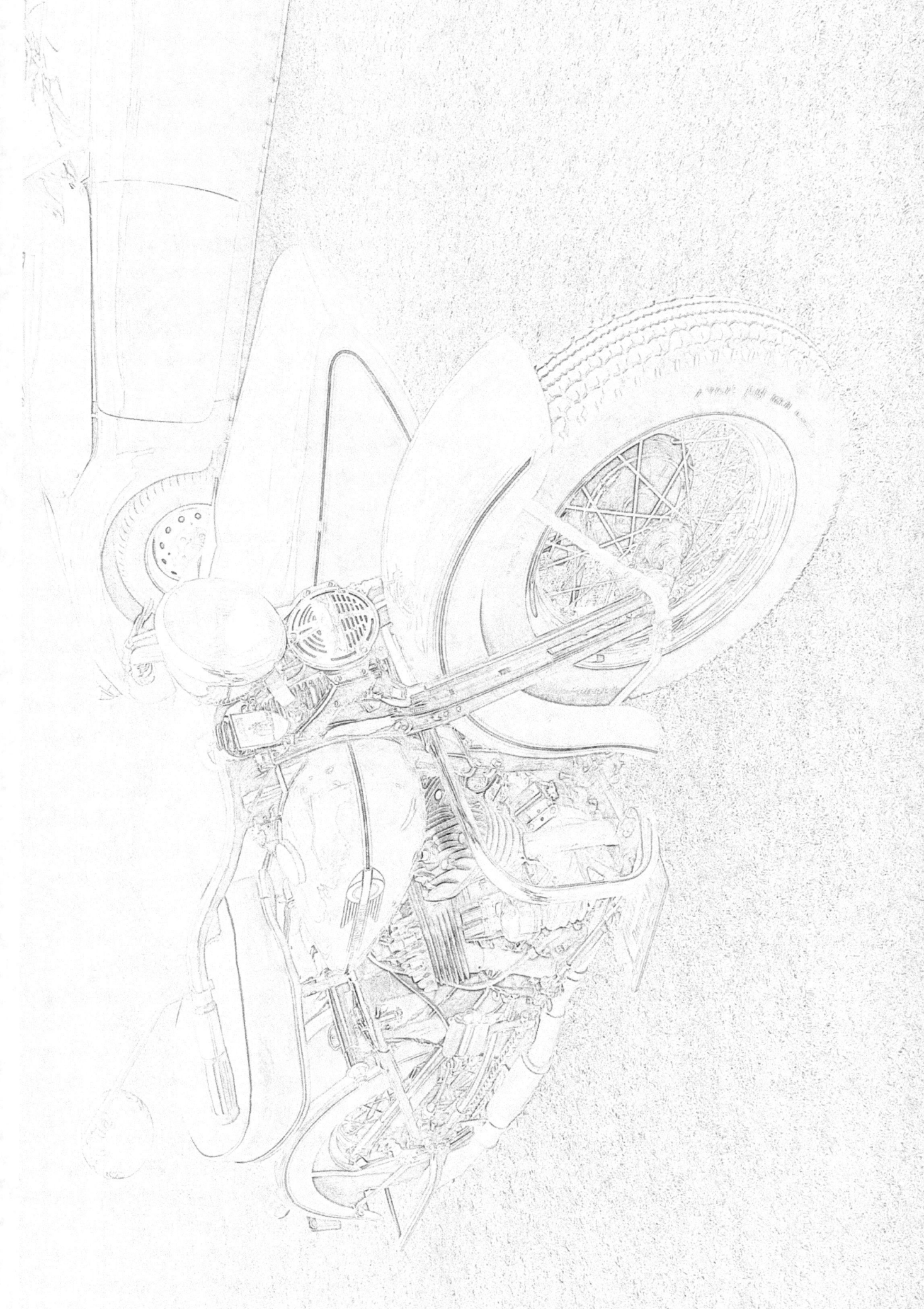

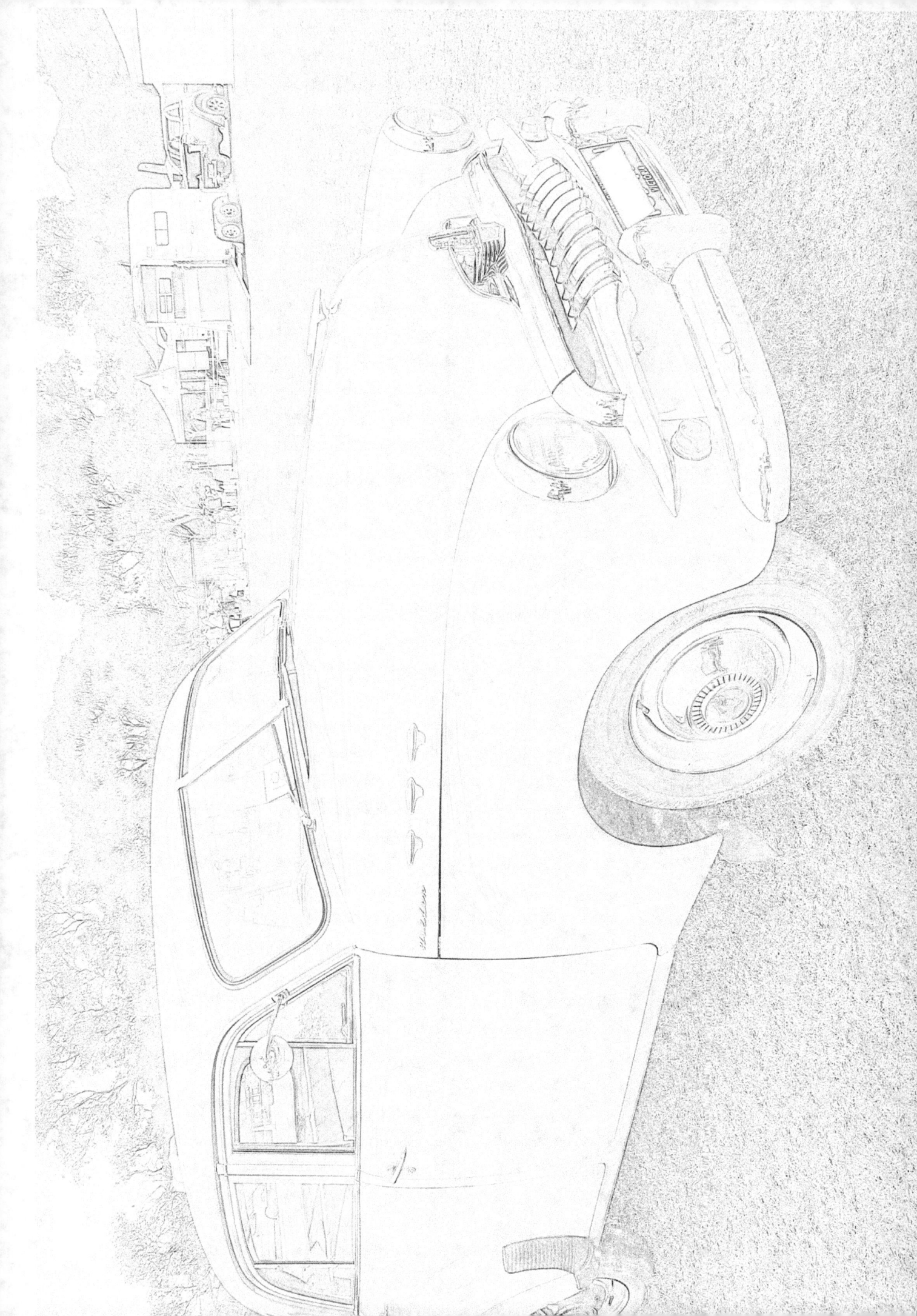

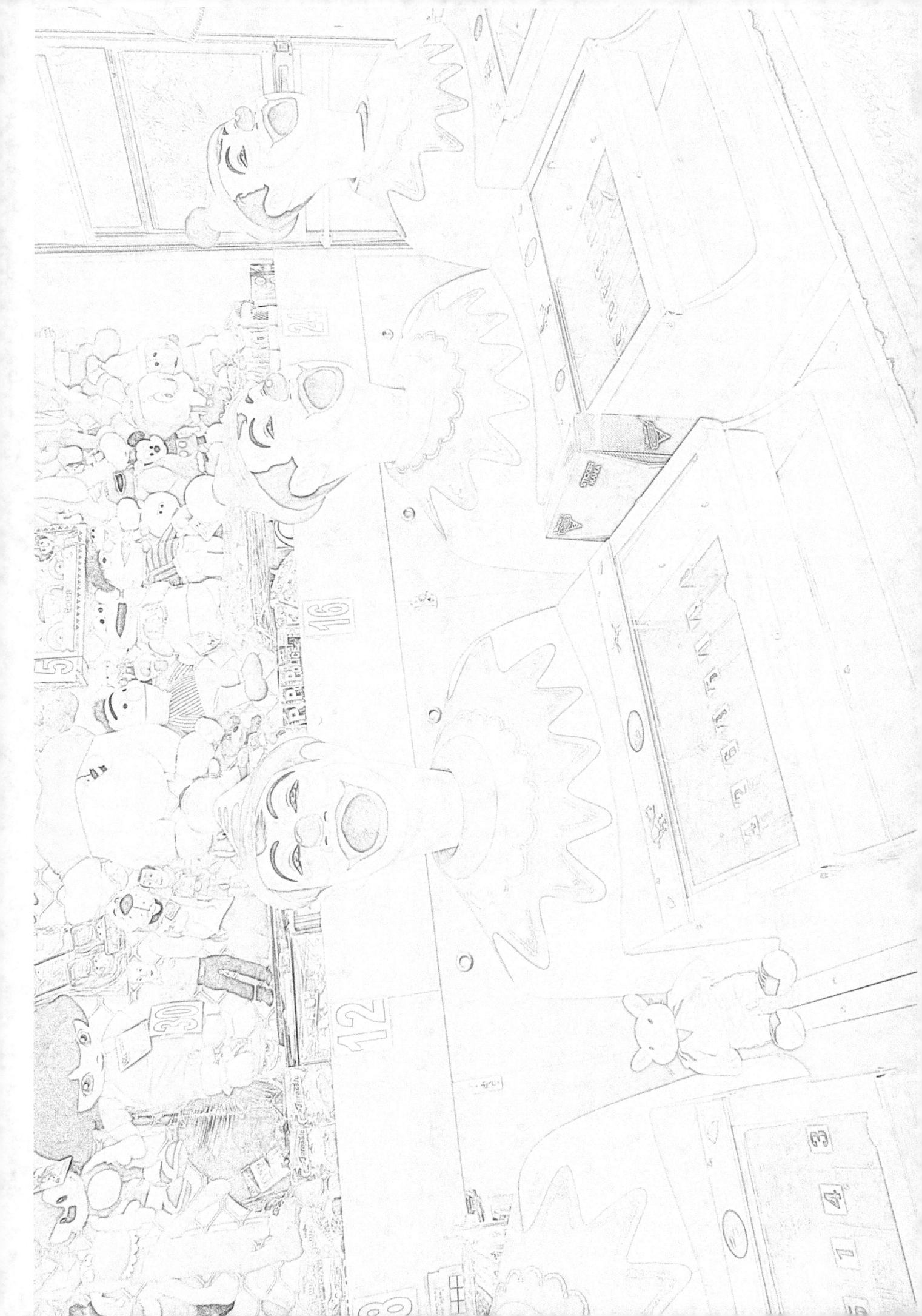

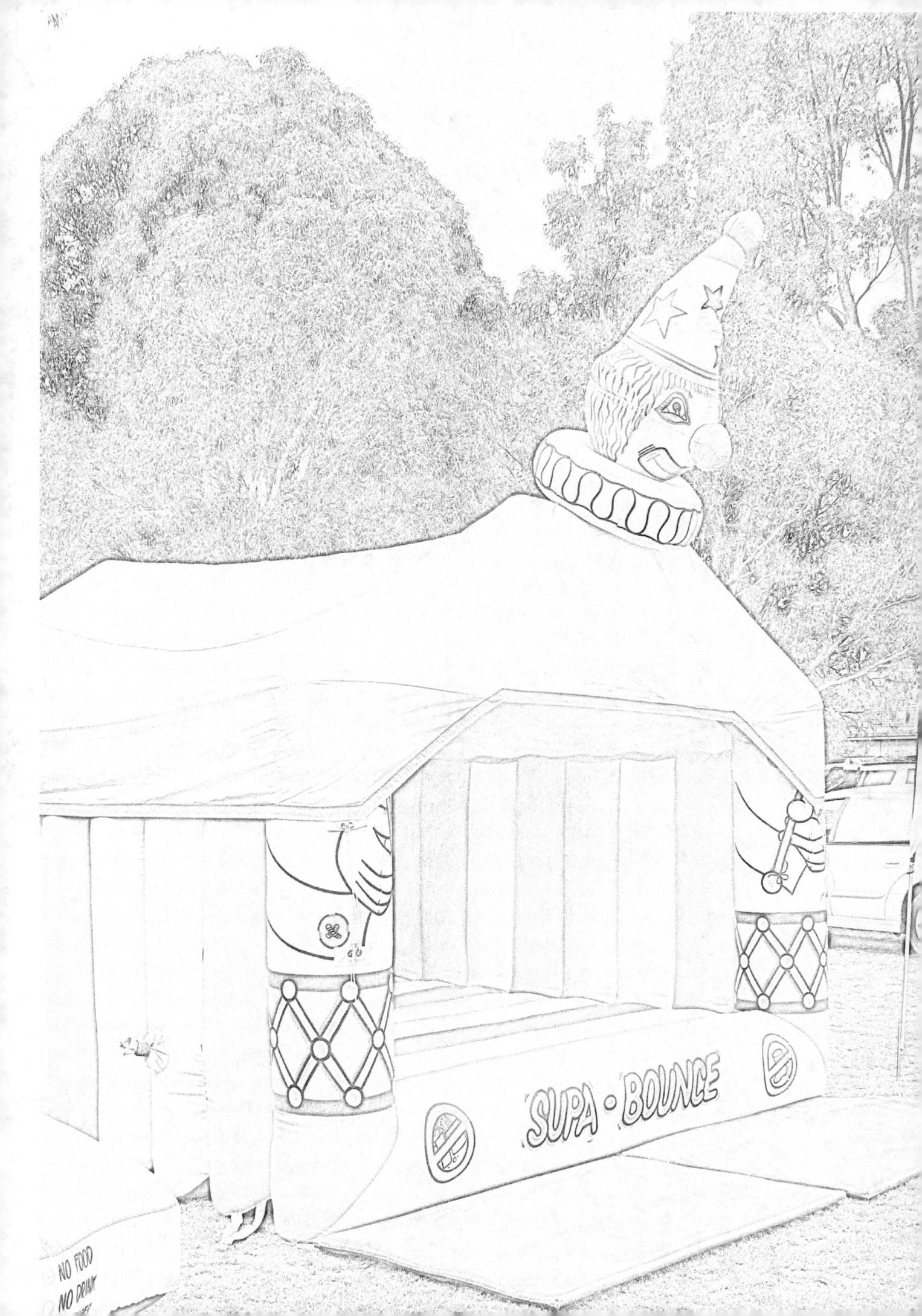

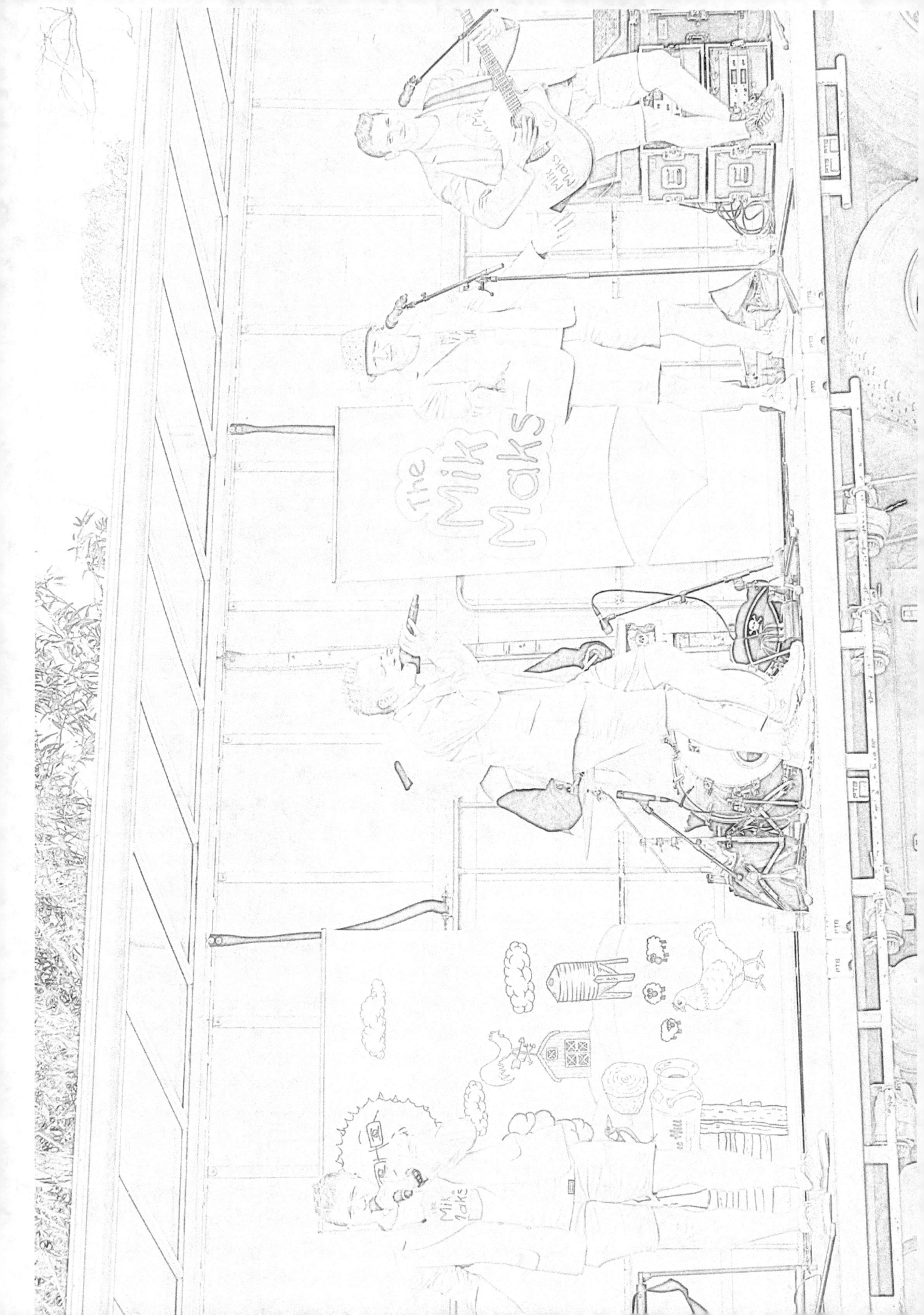

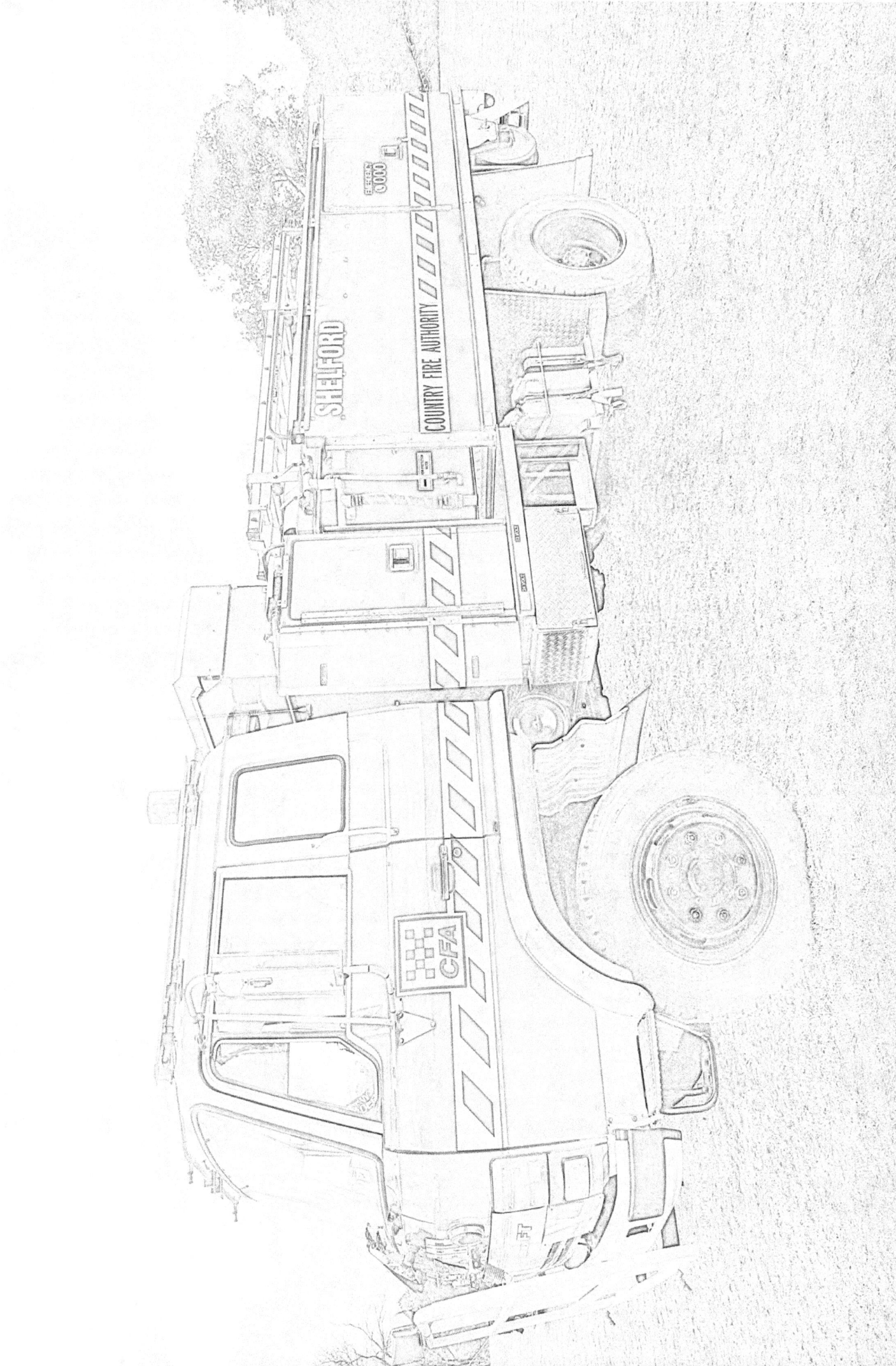

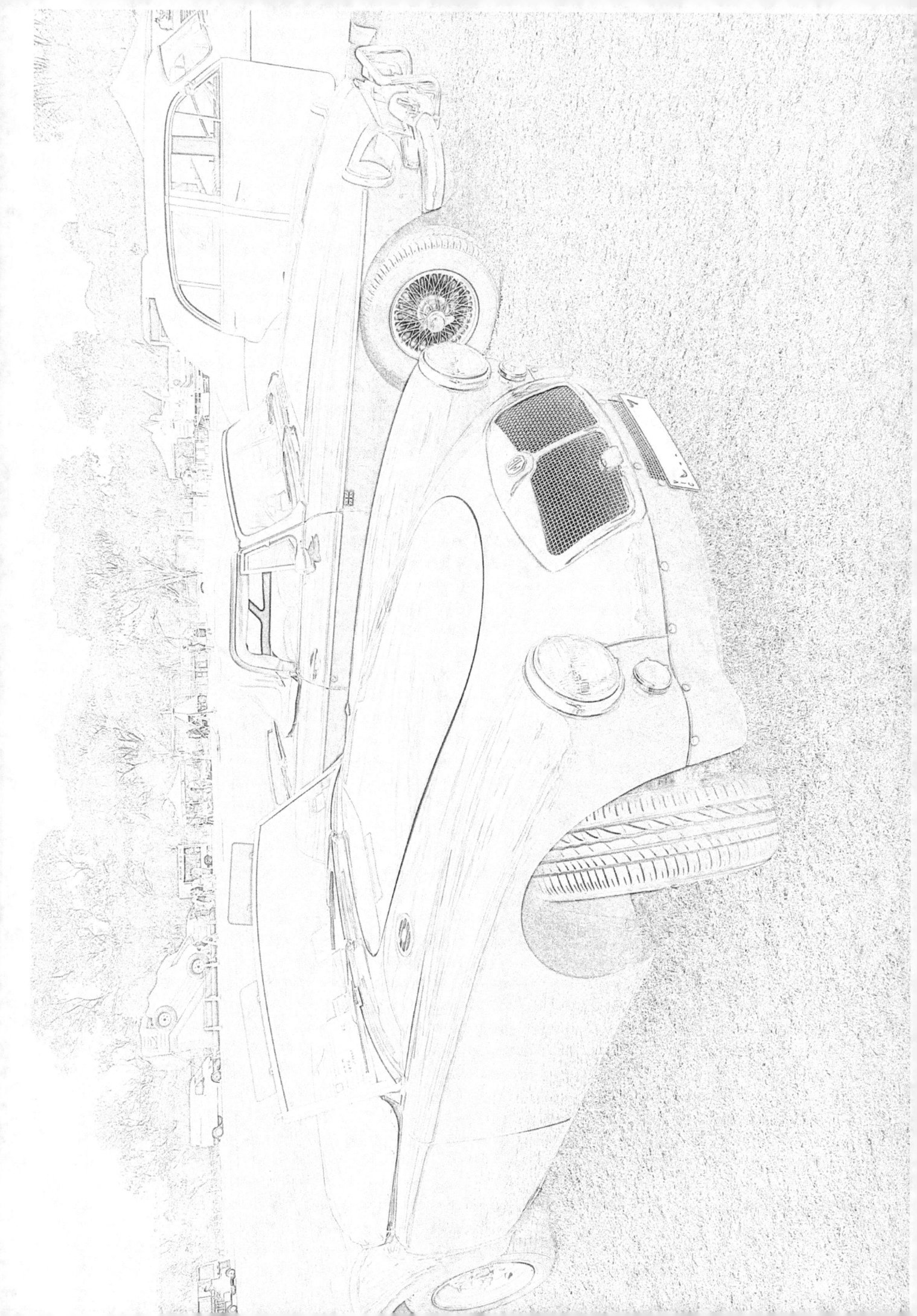

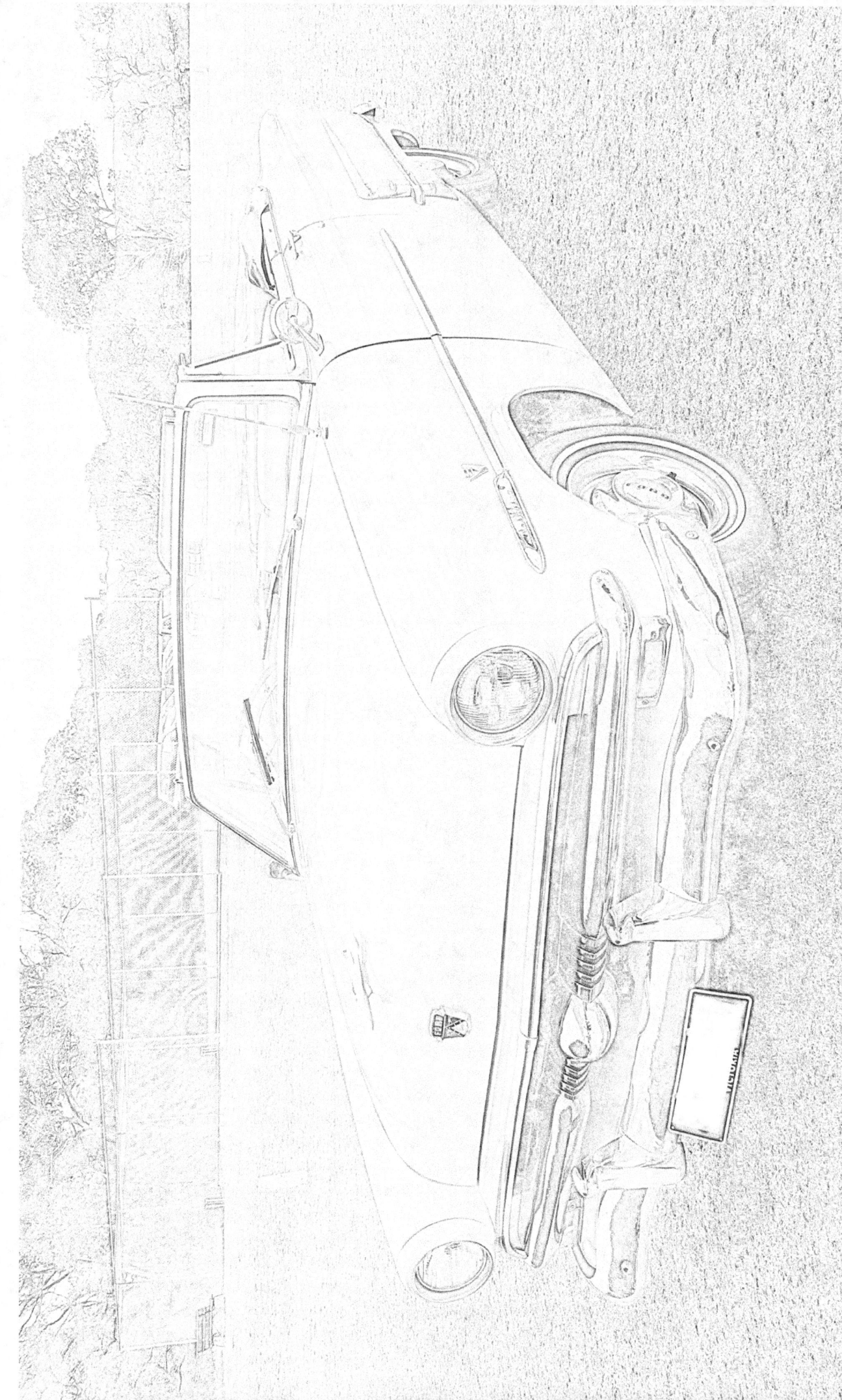

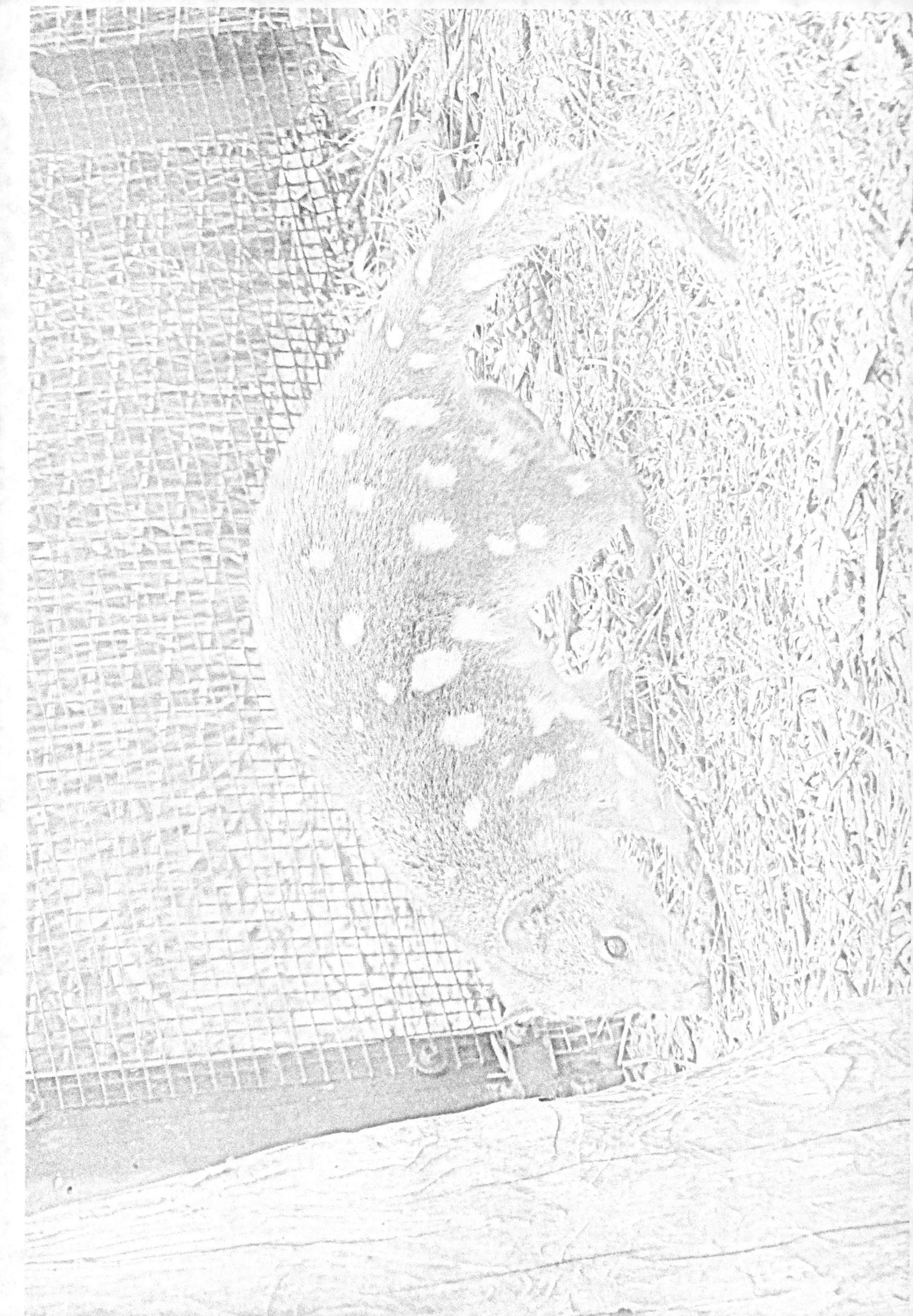

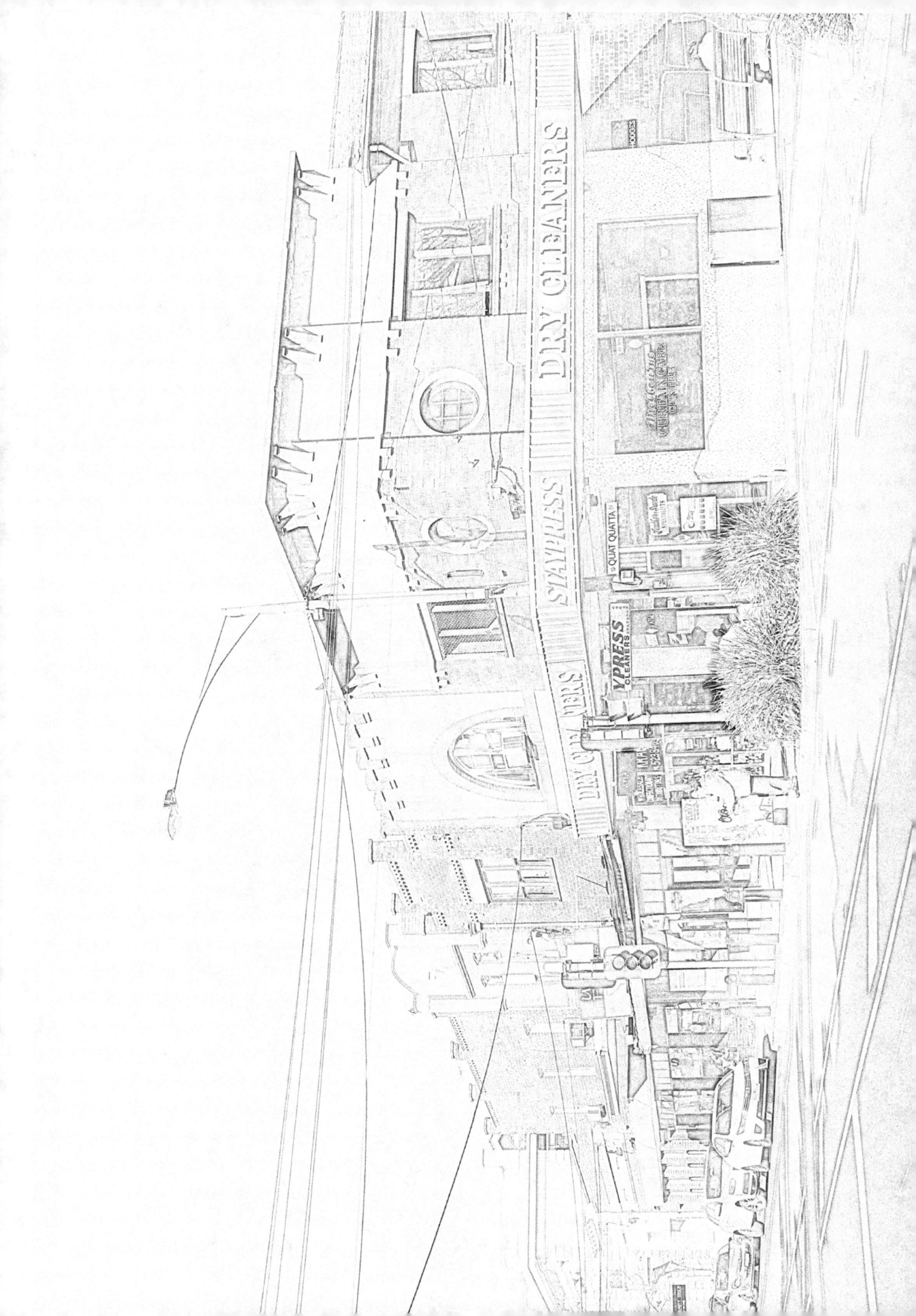

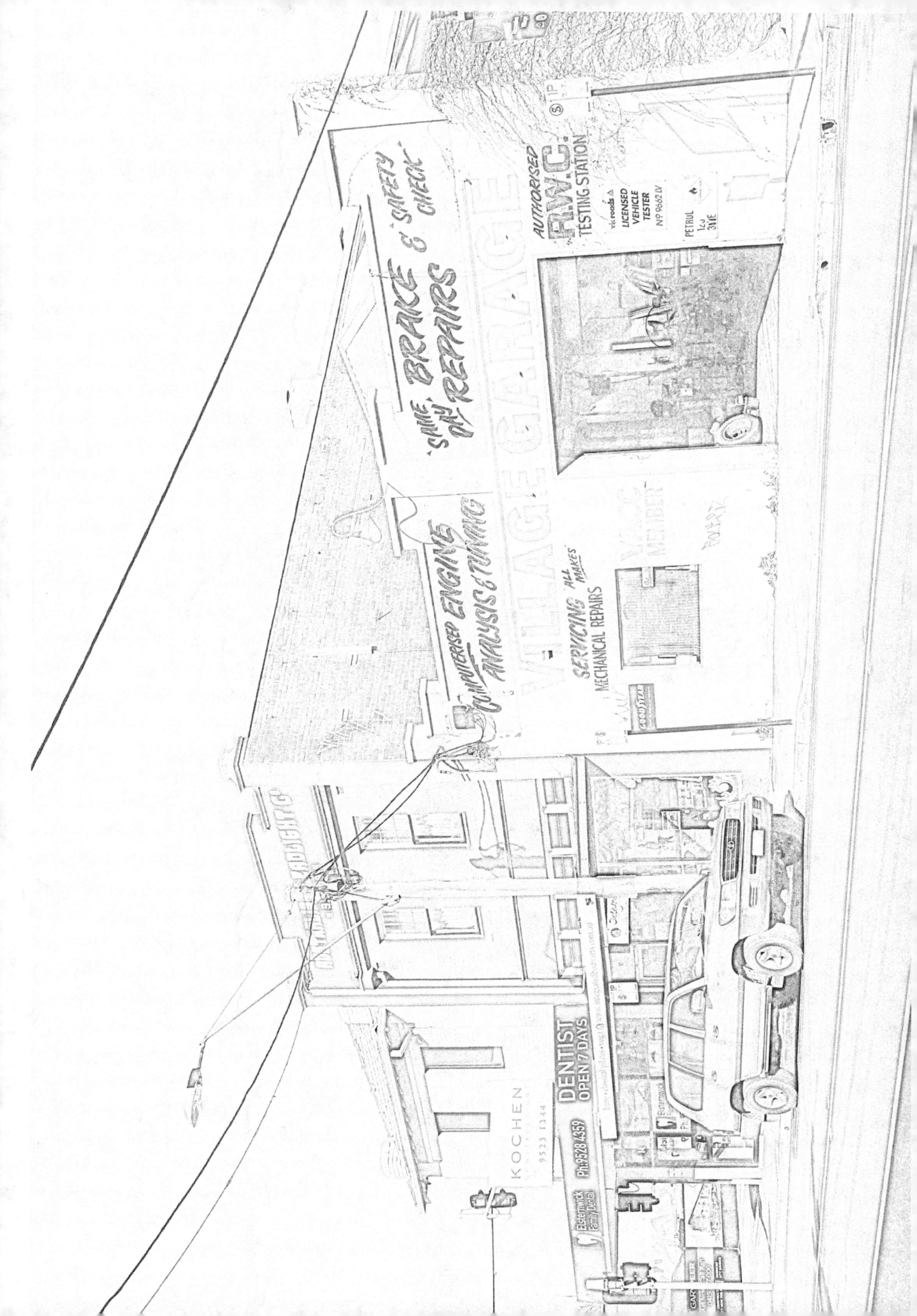

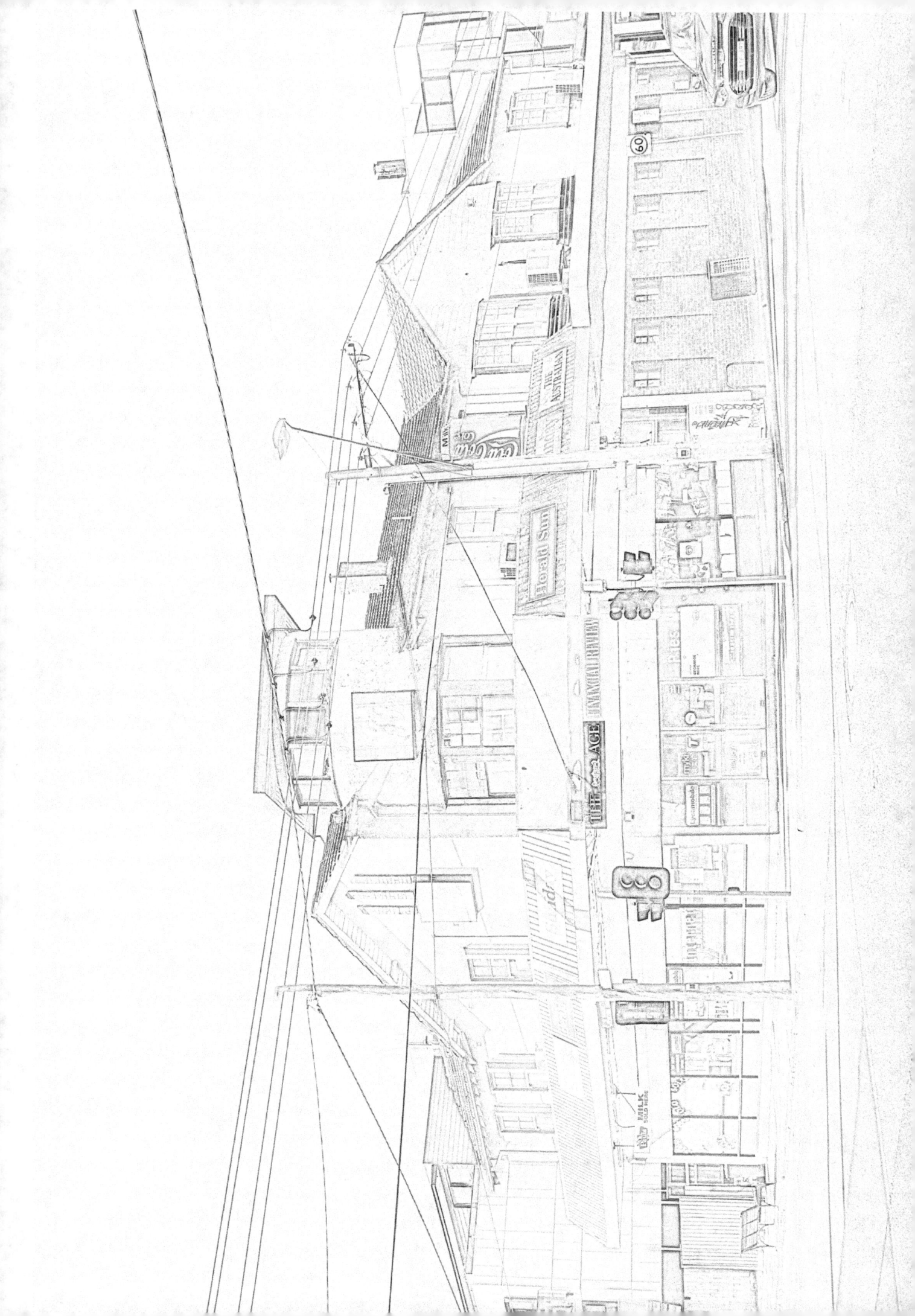

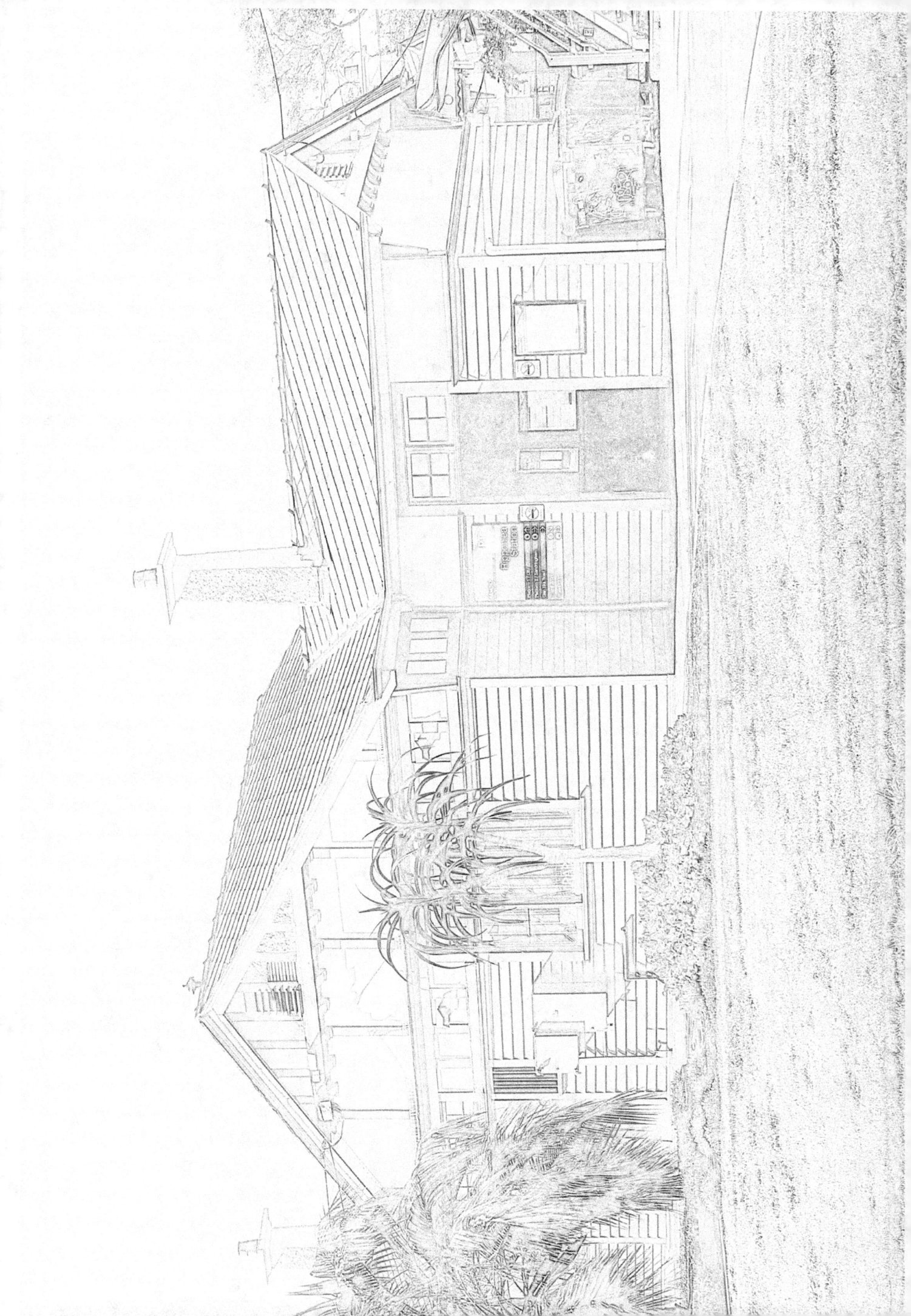

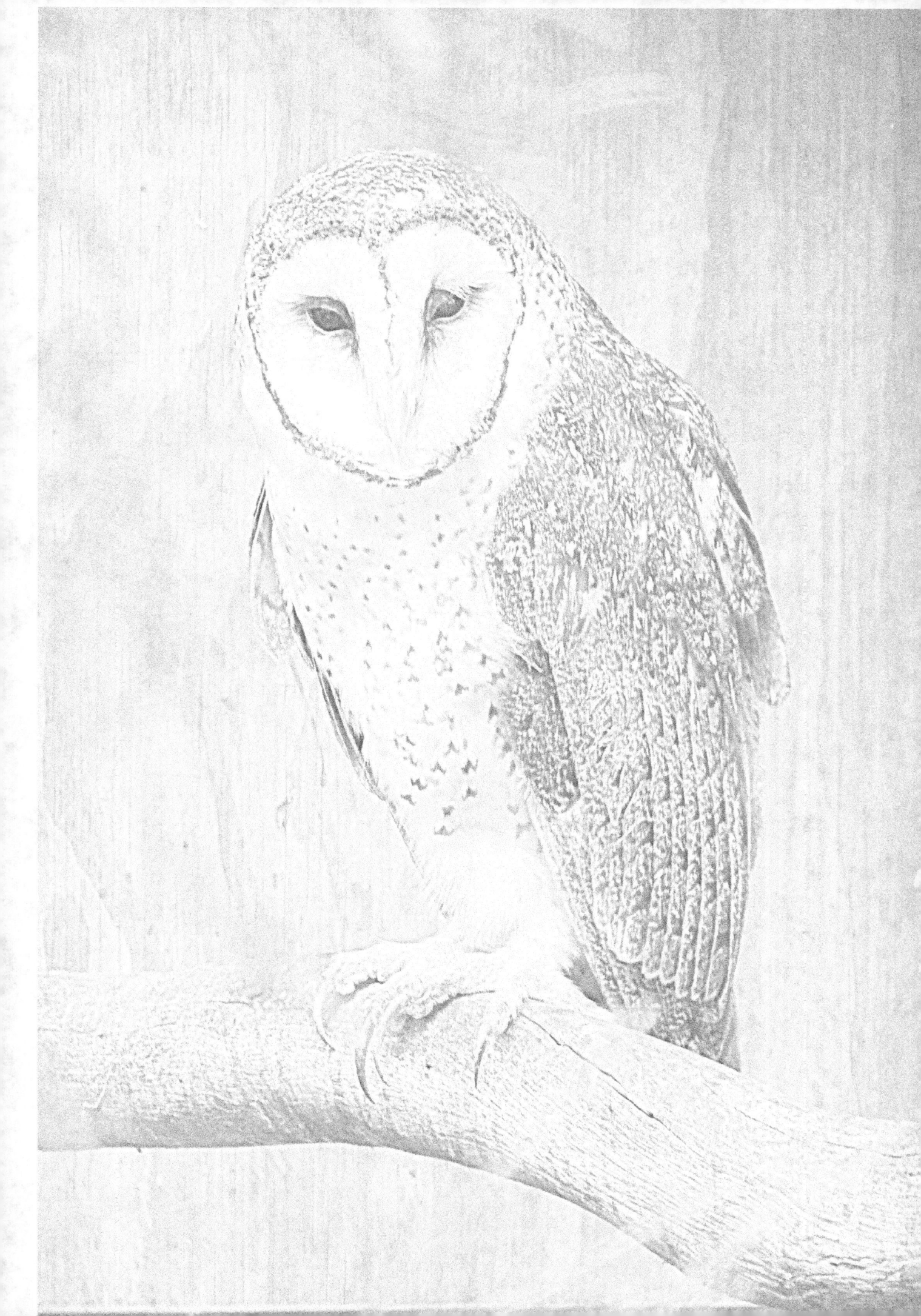

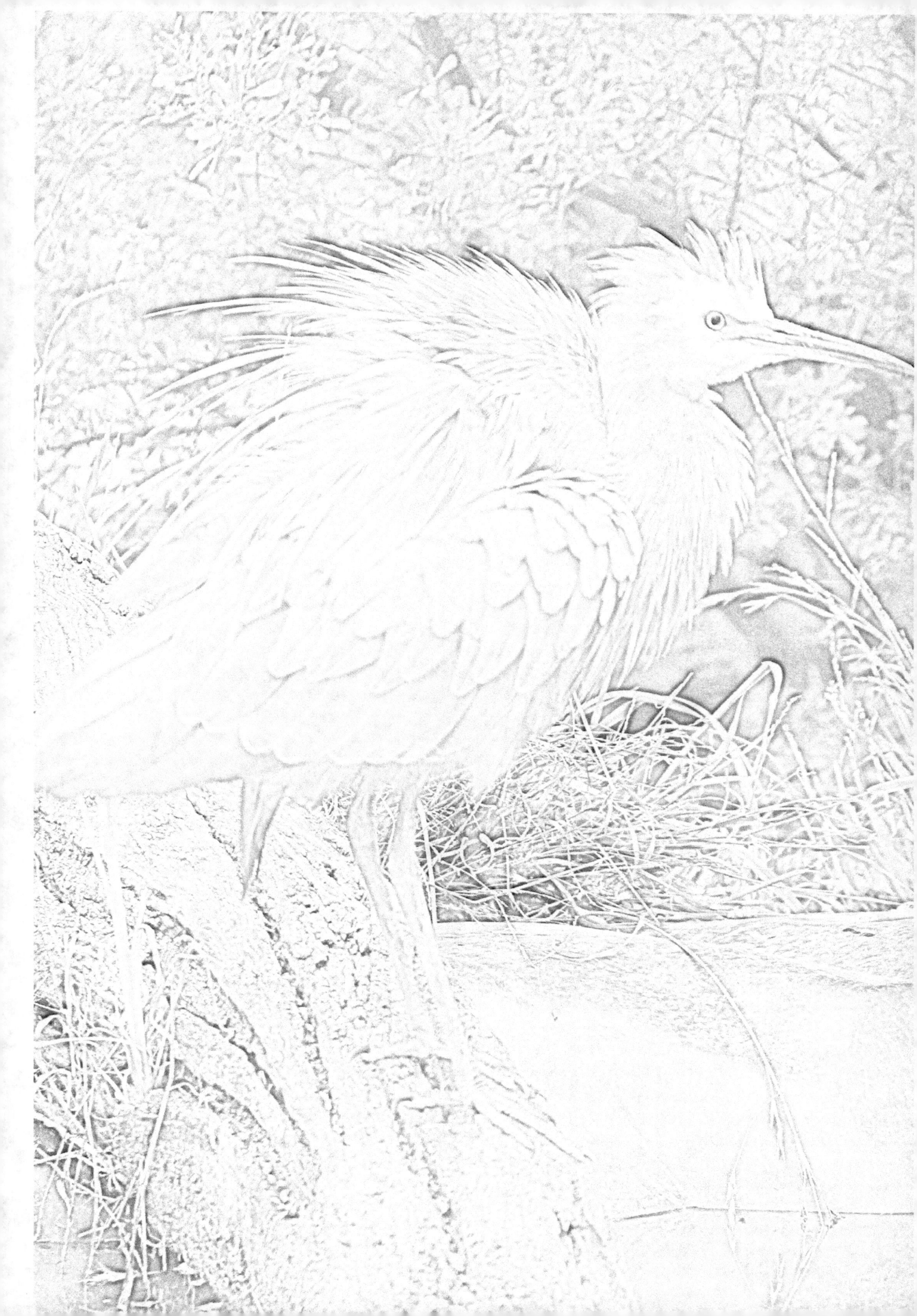

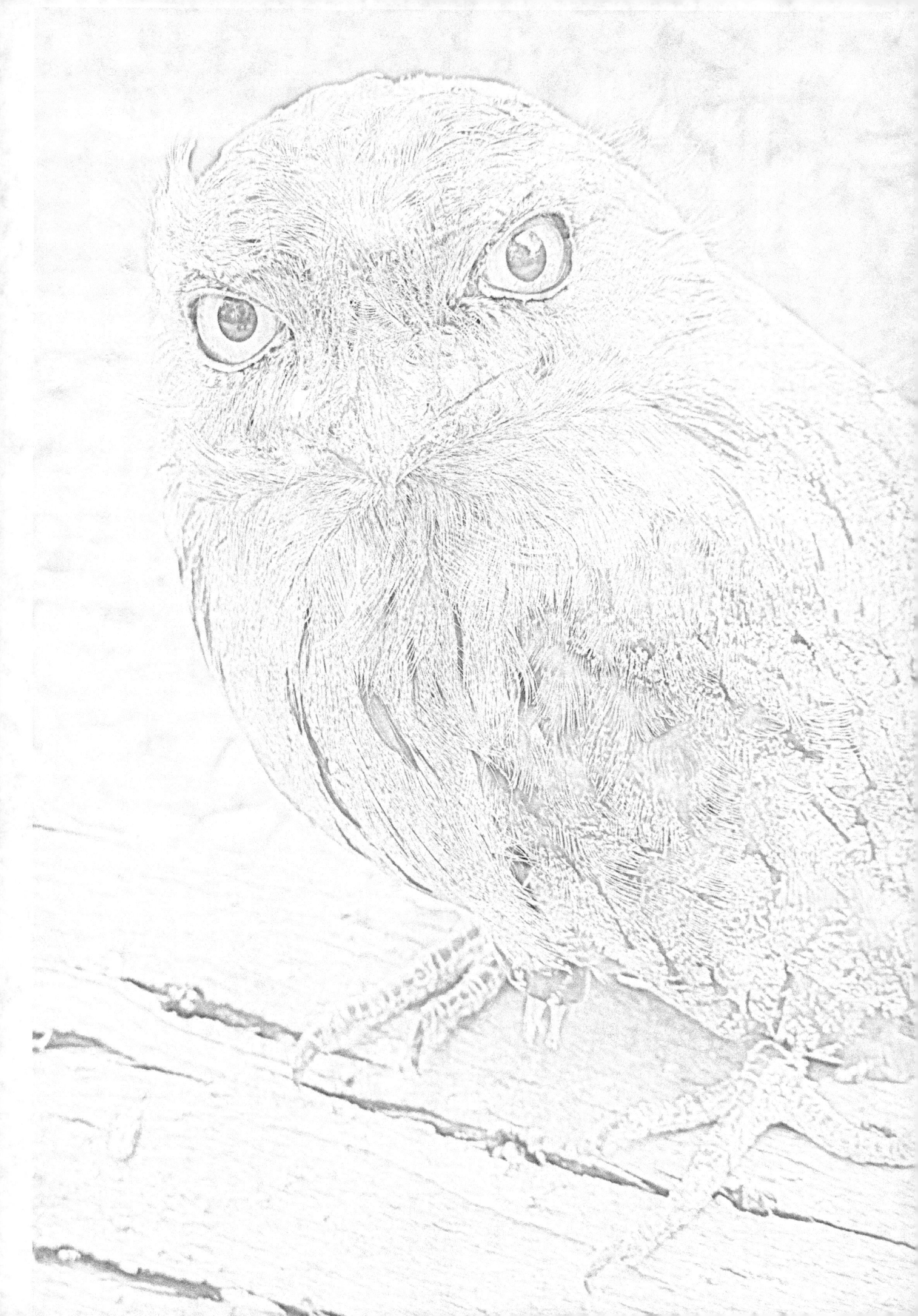

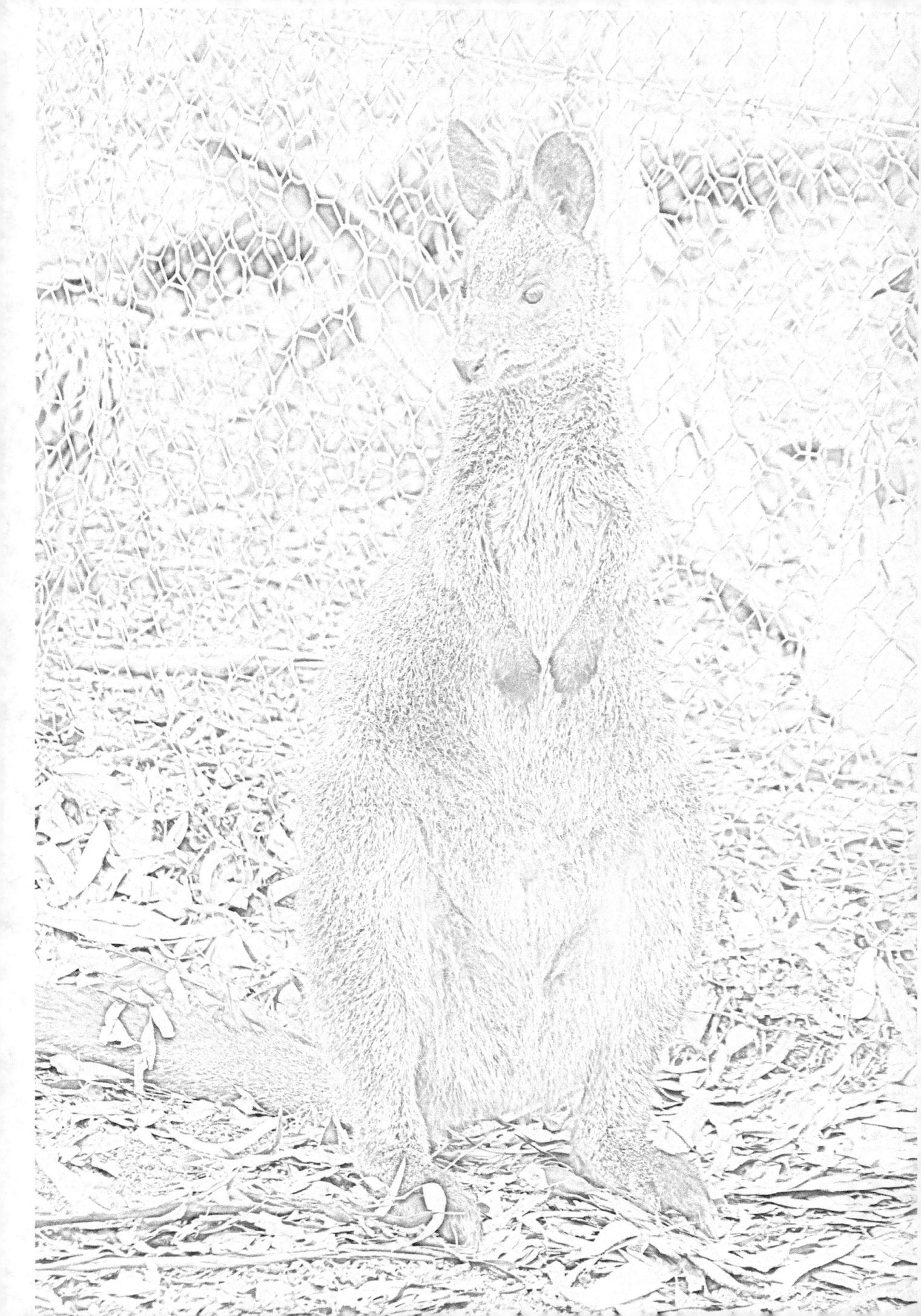

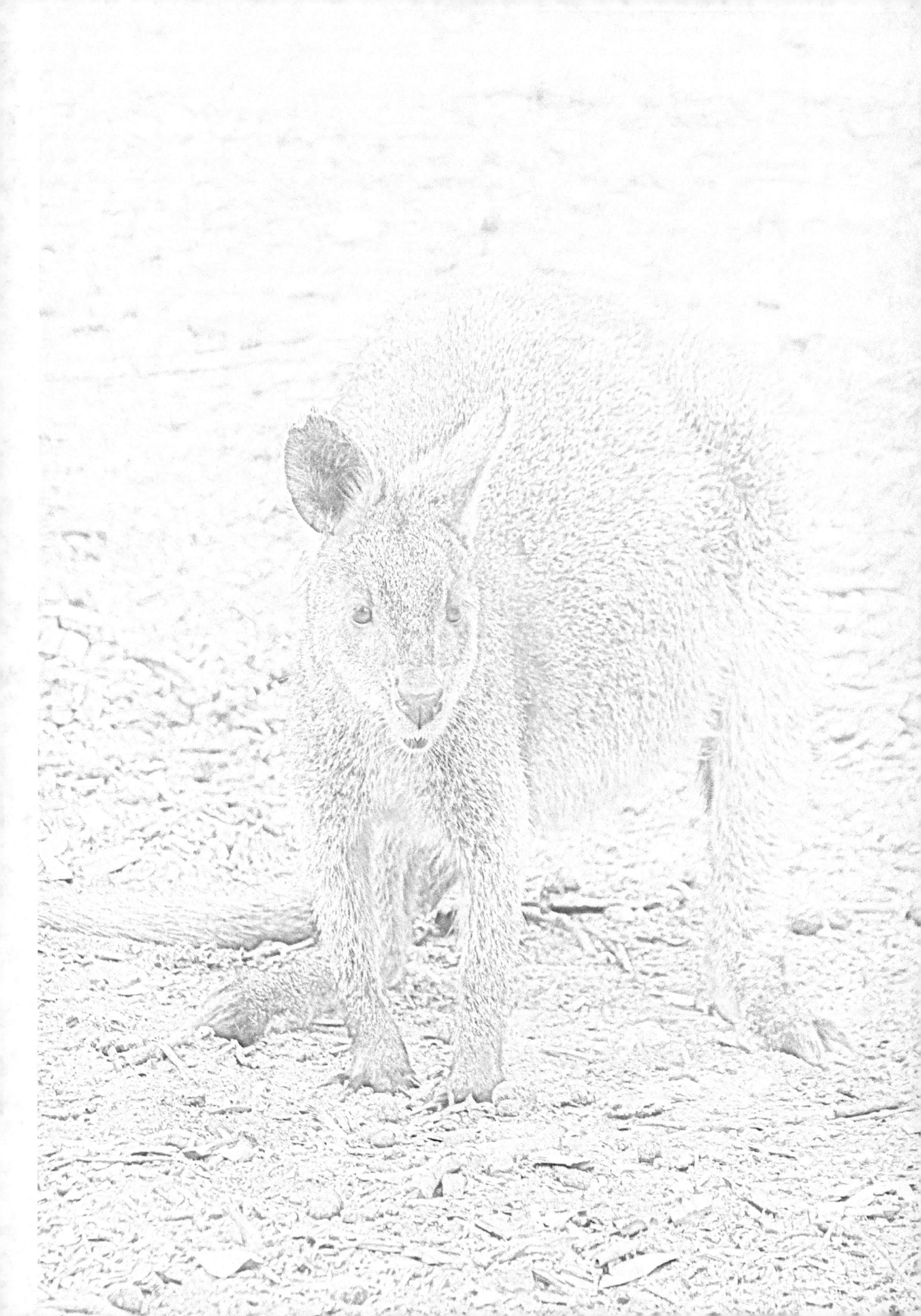

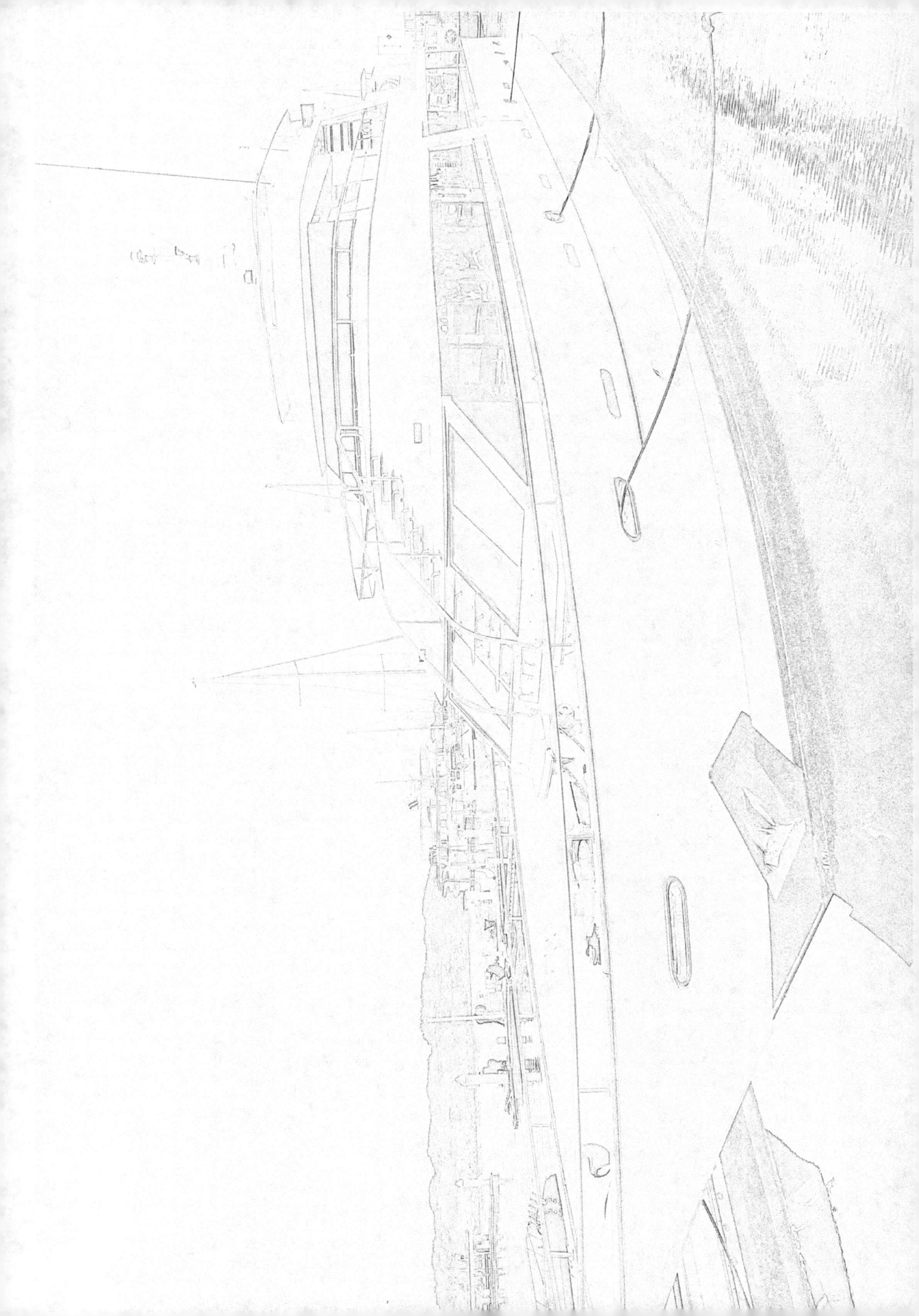

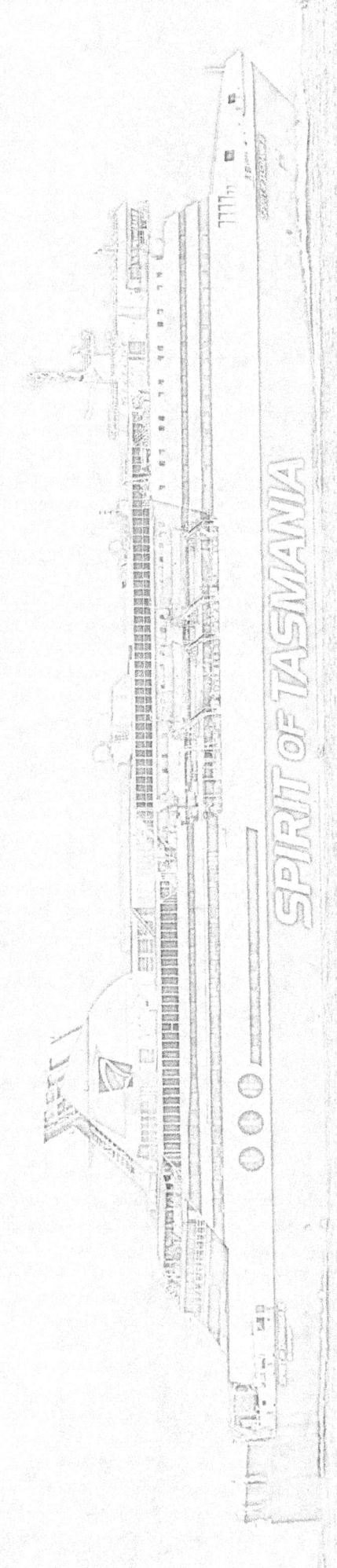

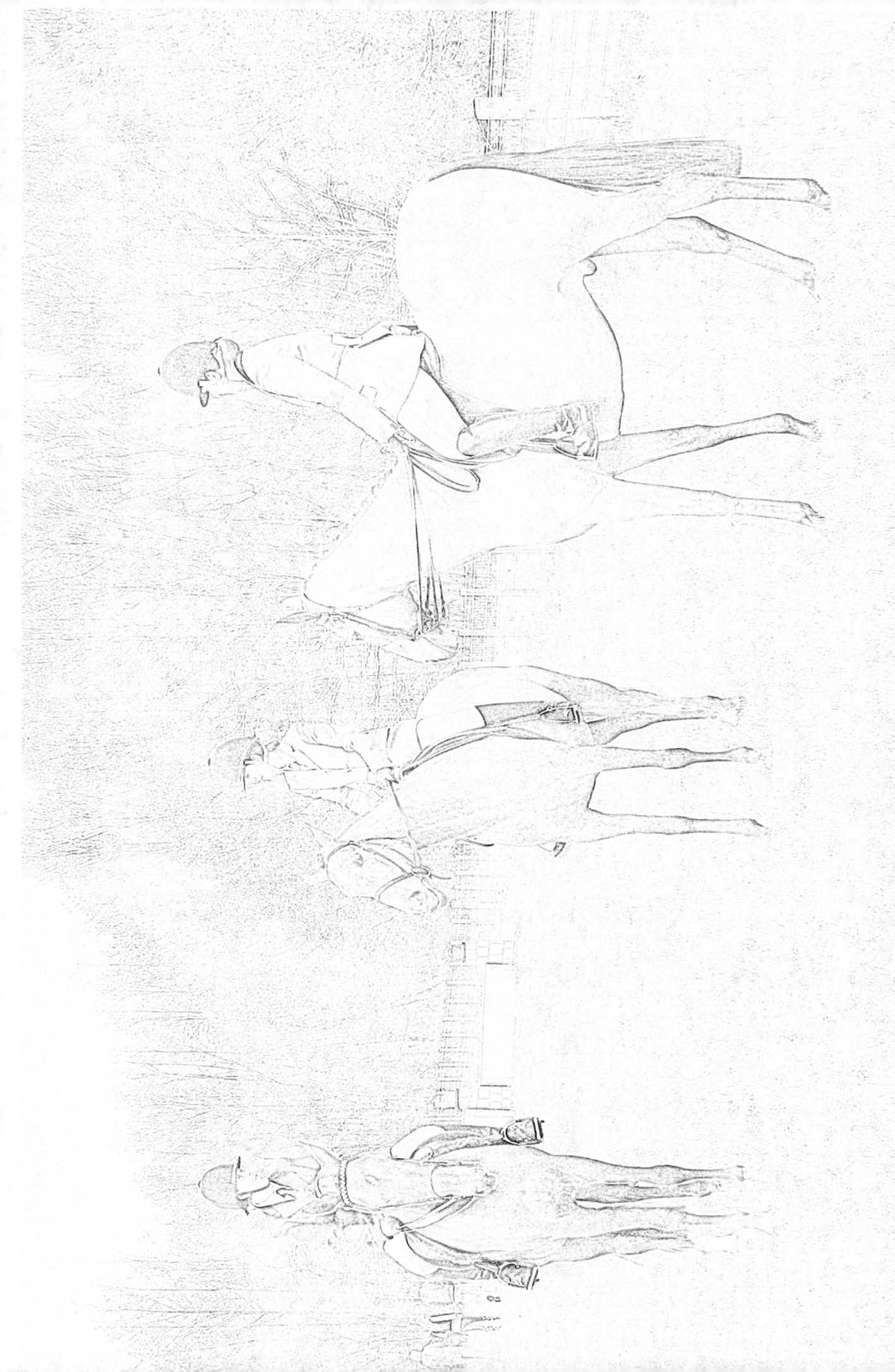

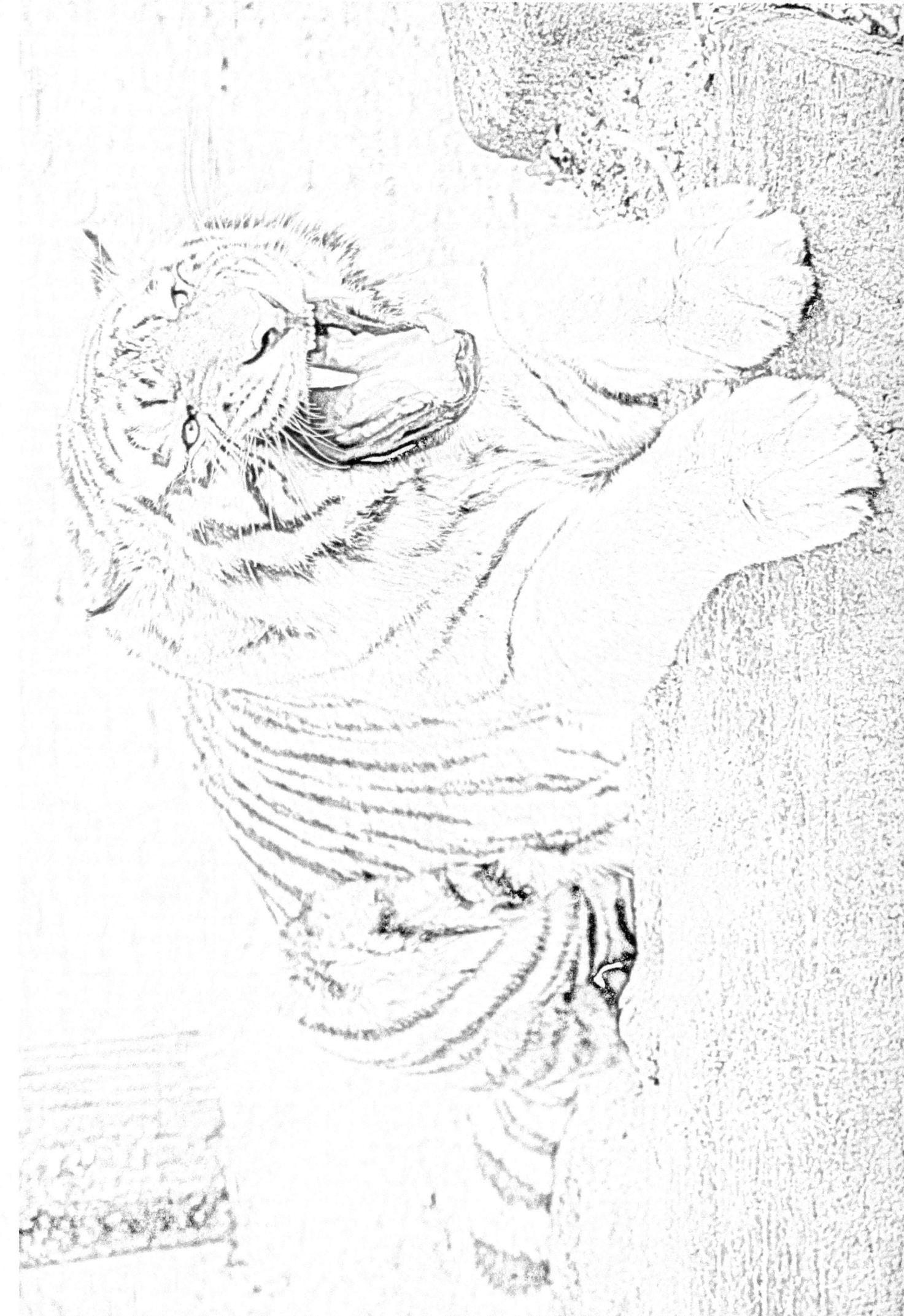

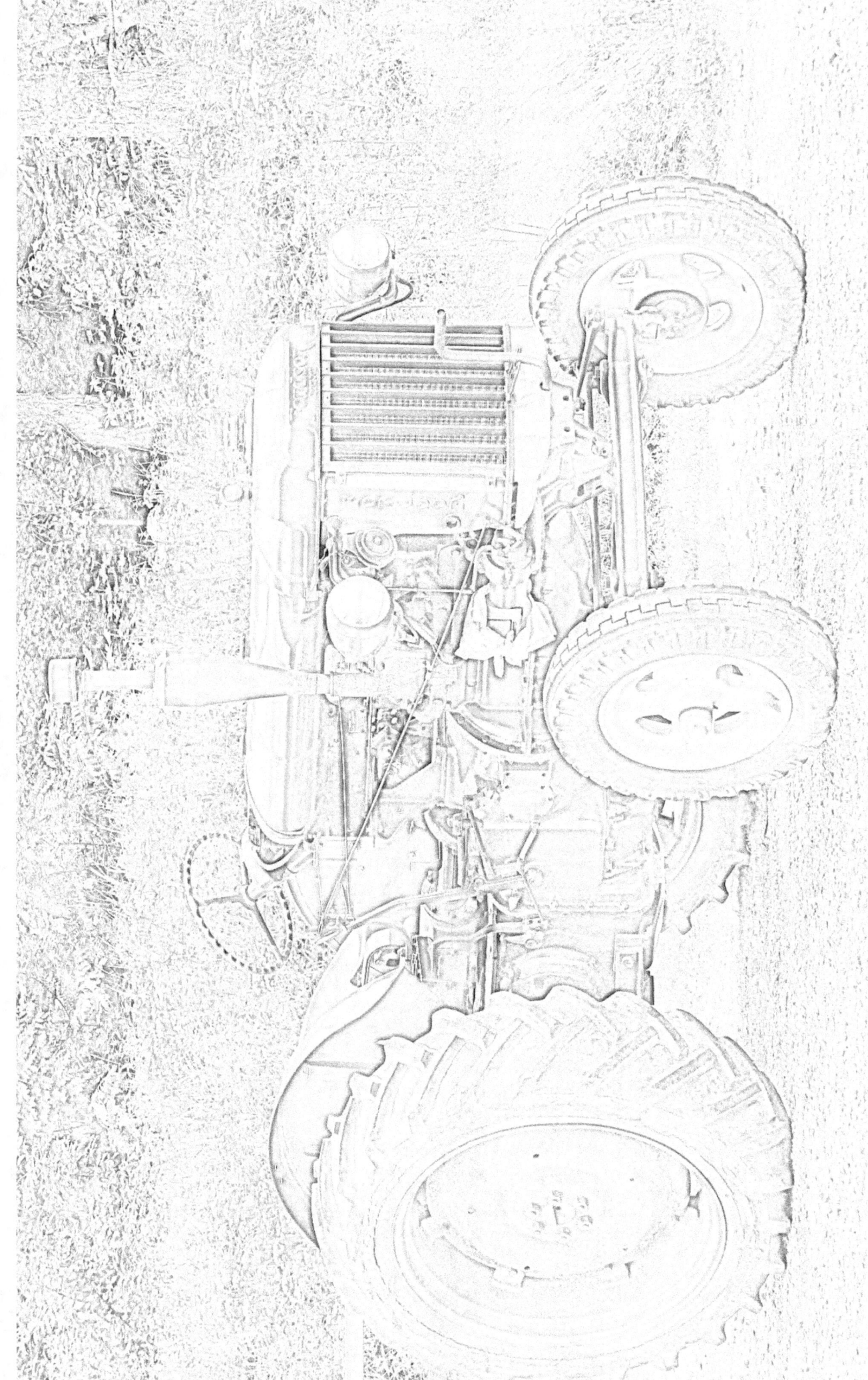

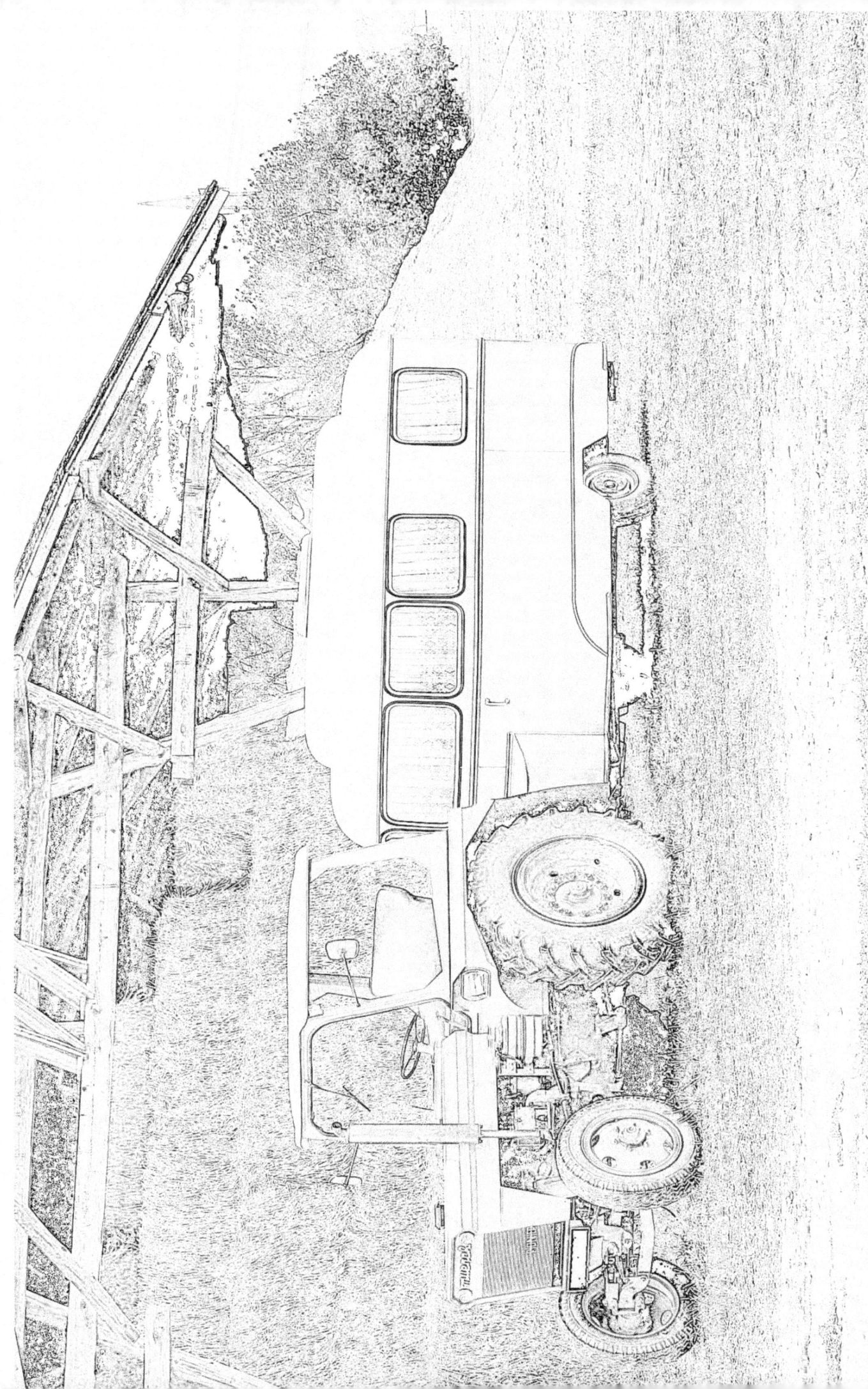

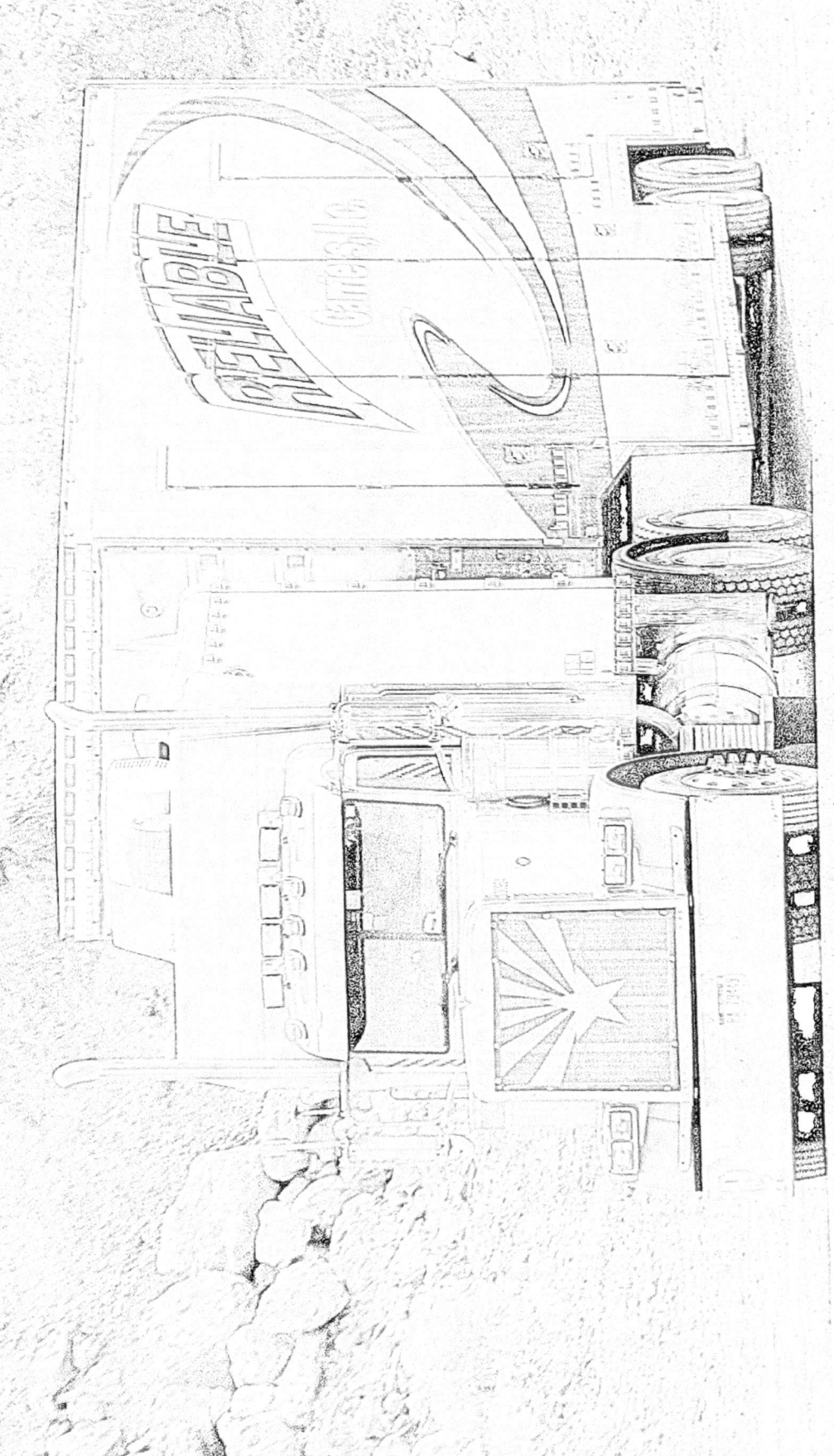

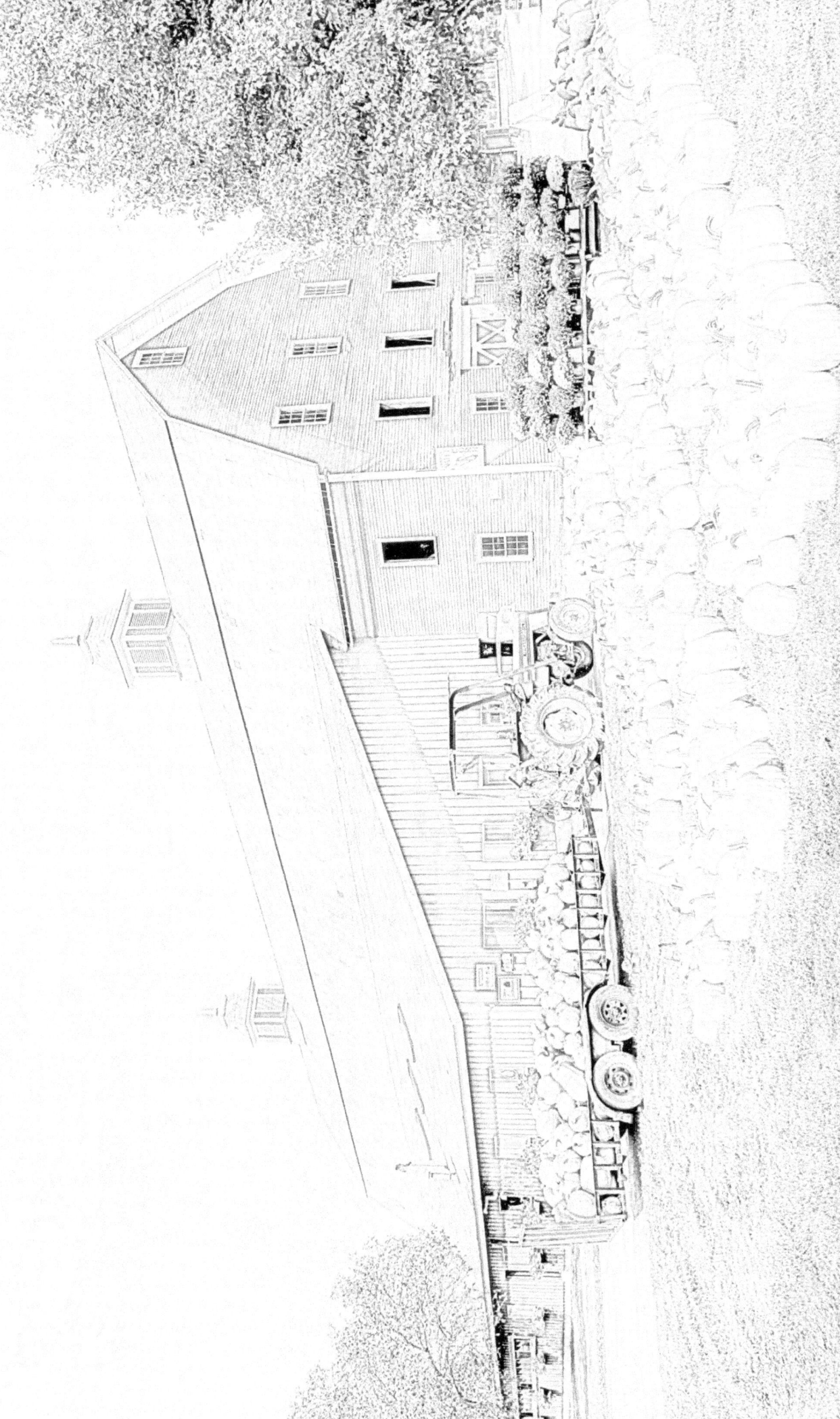

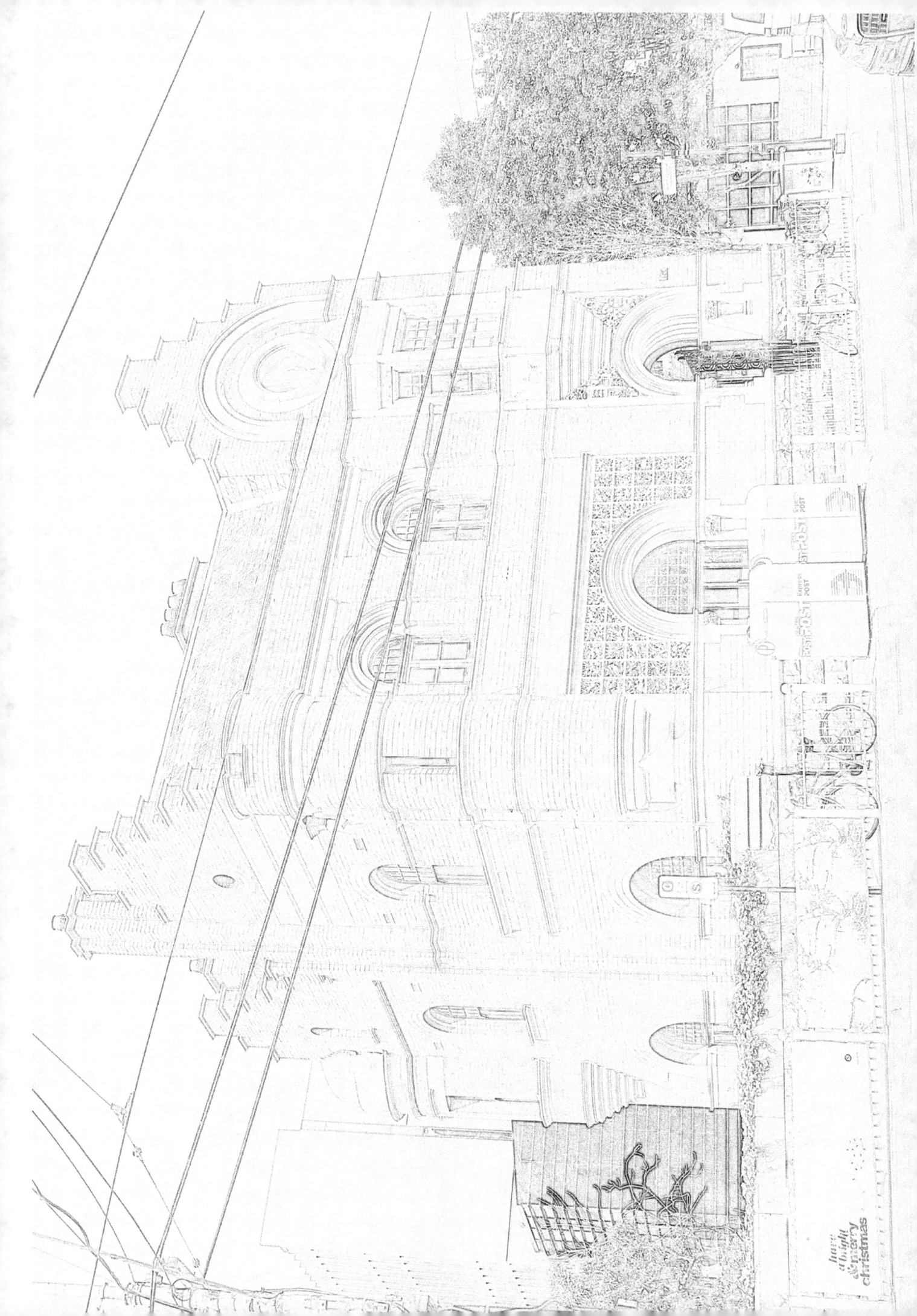

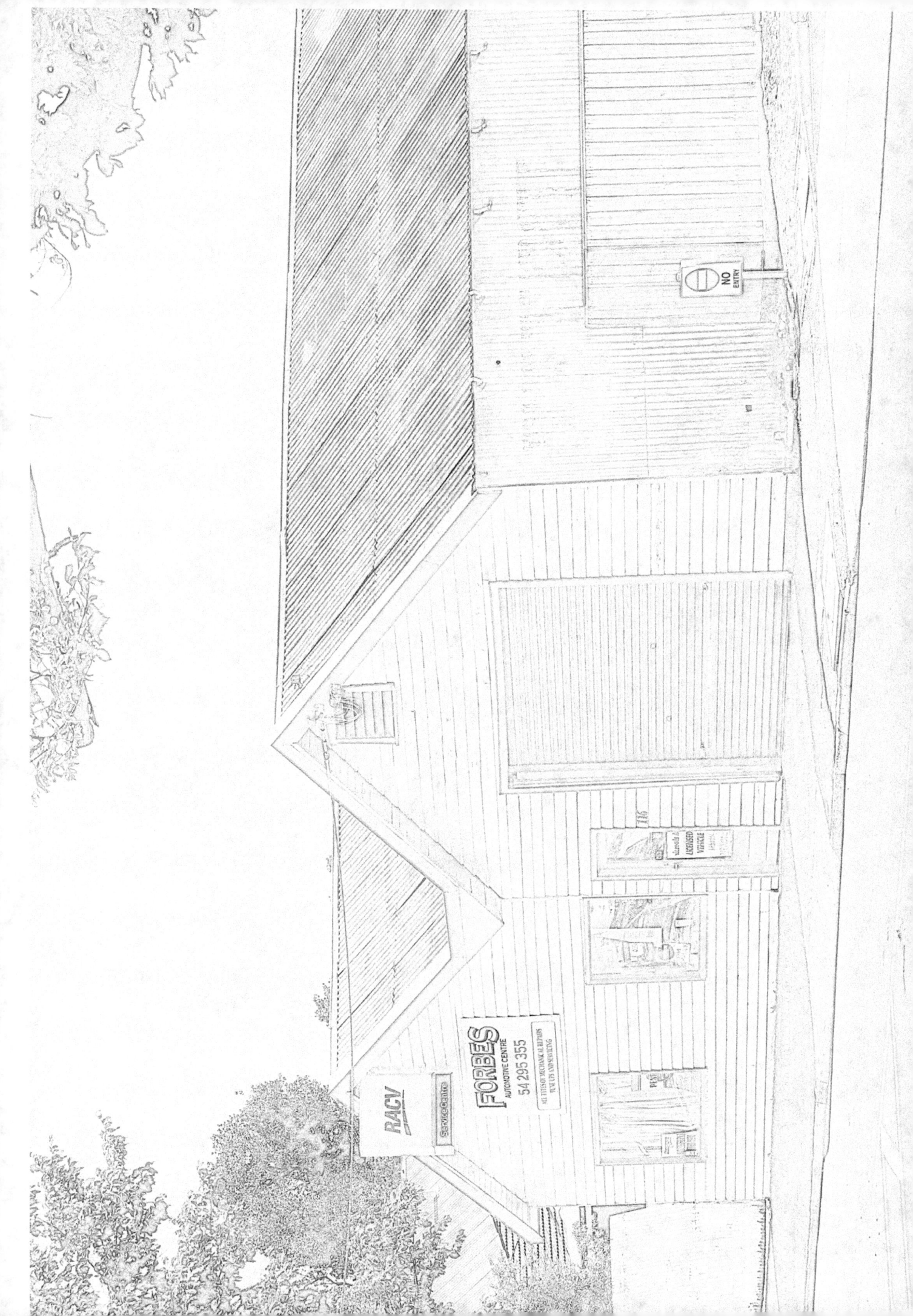

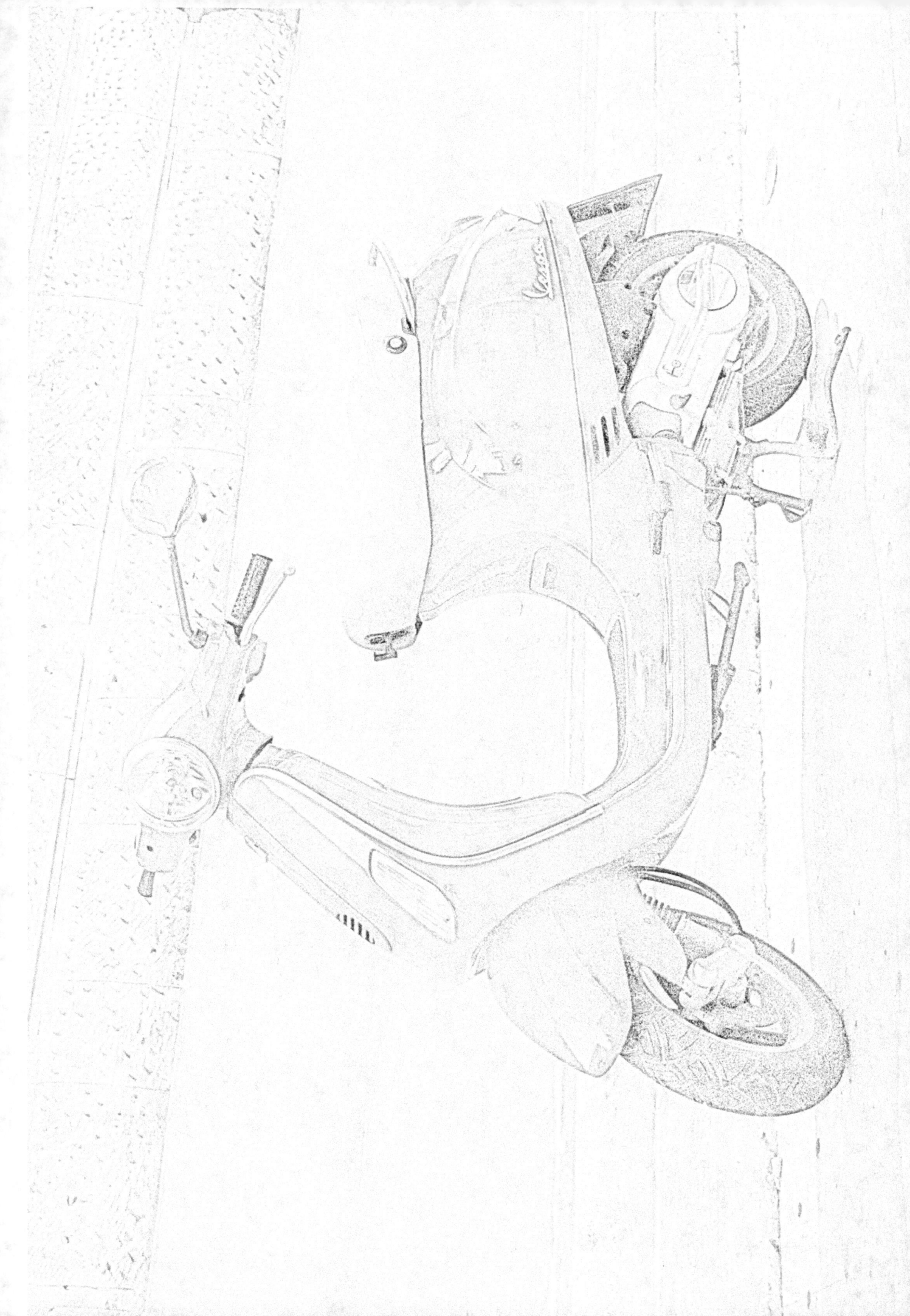

www.ingramcontent.com/pod-product-compliance
Lightning Source LLC
Chambersburg PA
CBHW081056180526
45170CB00005B/1776

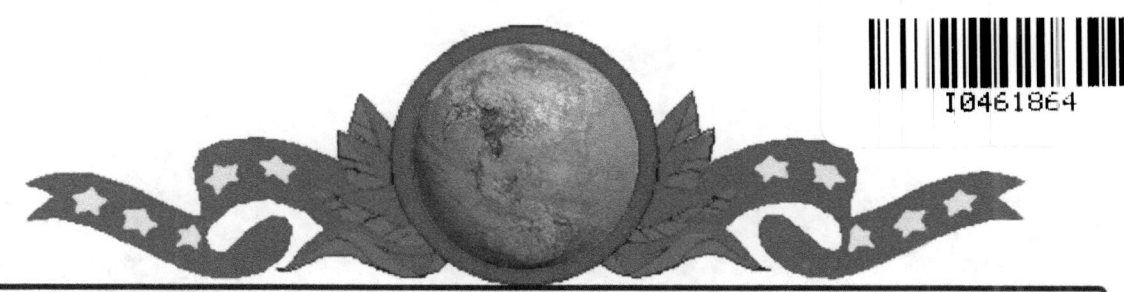

# Real World
## Colouring Book
### For Advanced Users & Adults

## 50 Images

## Created From Real Life Photos For You To Colour As You Please.

ISBN 978-0-359-83329-0

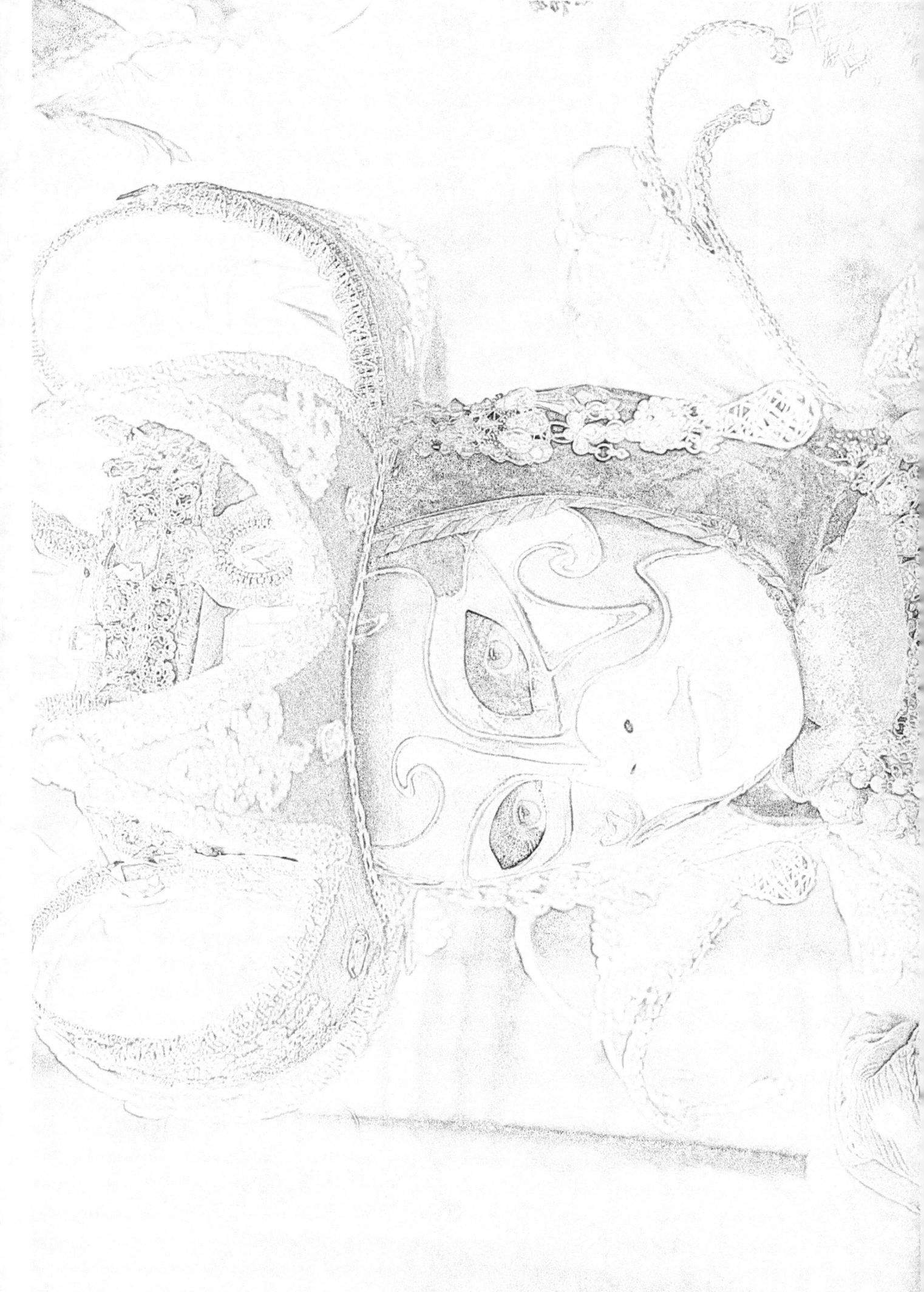

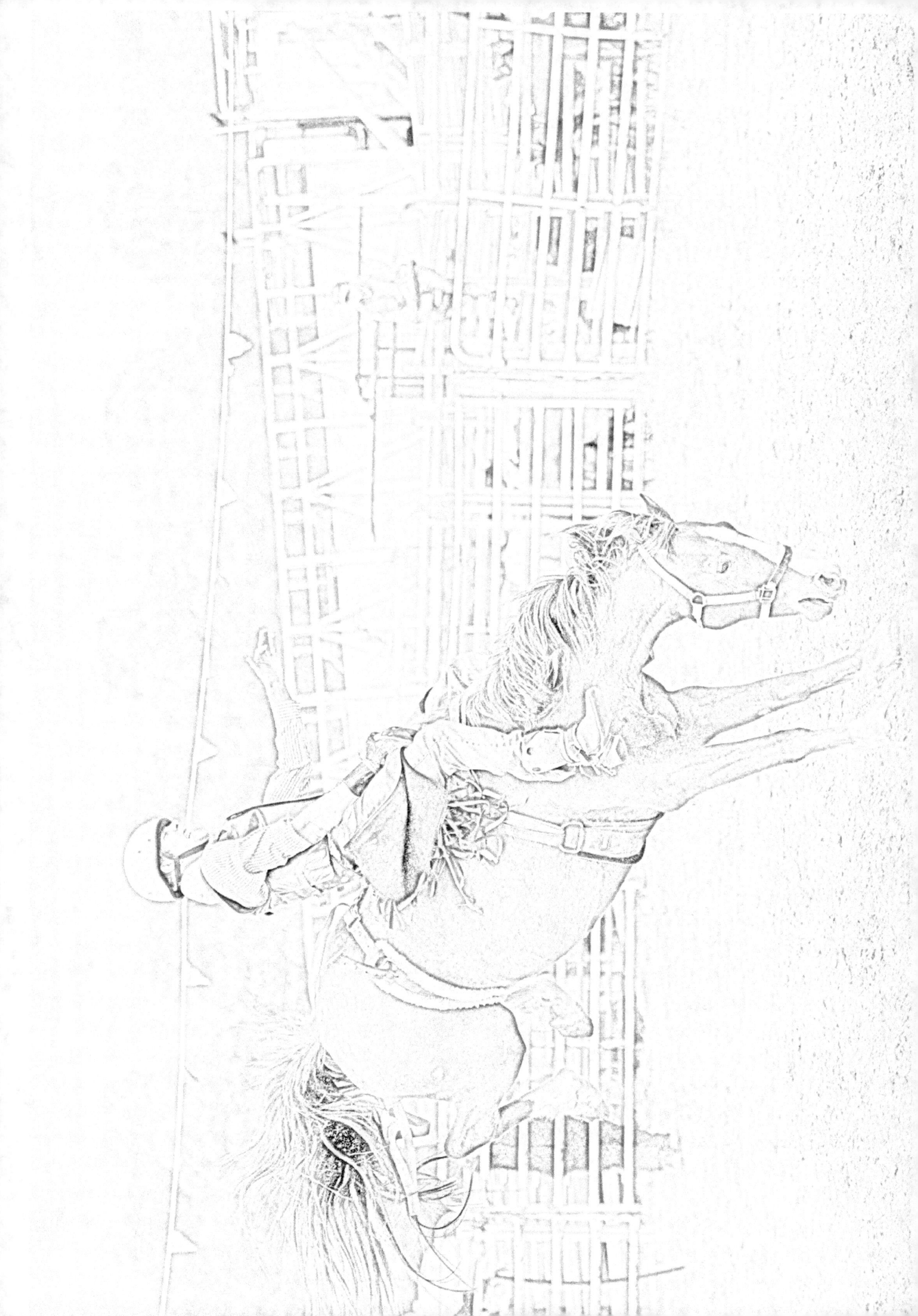

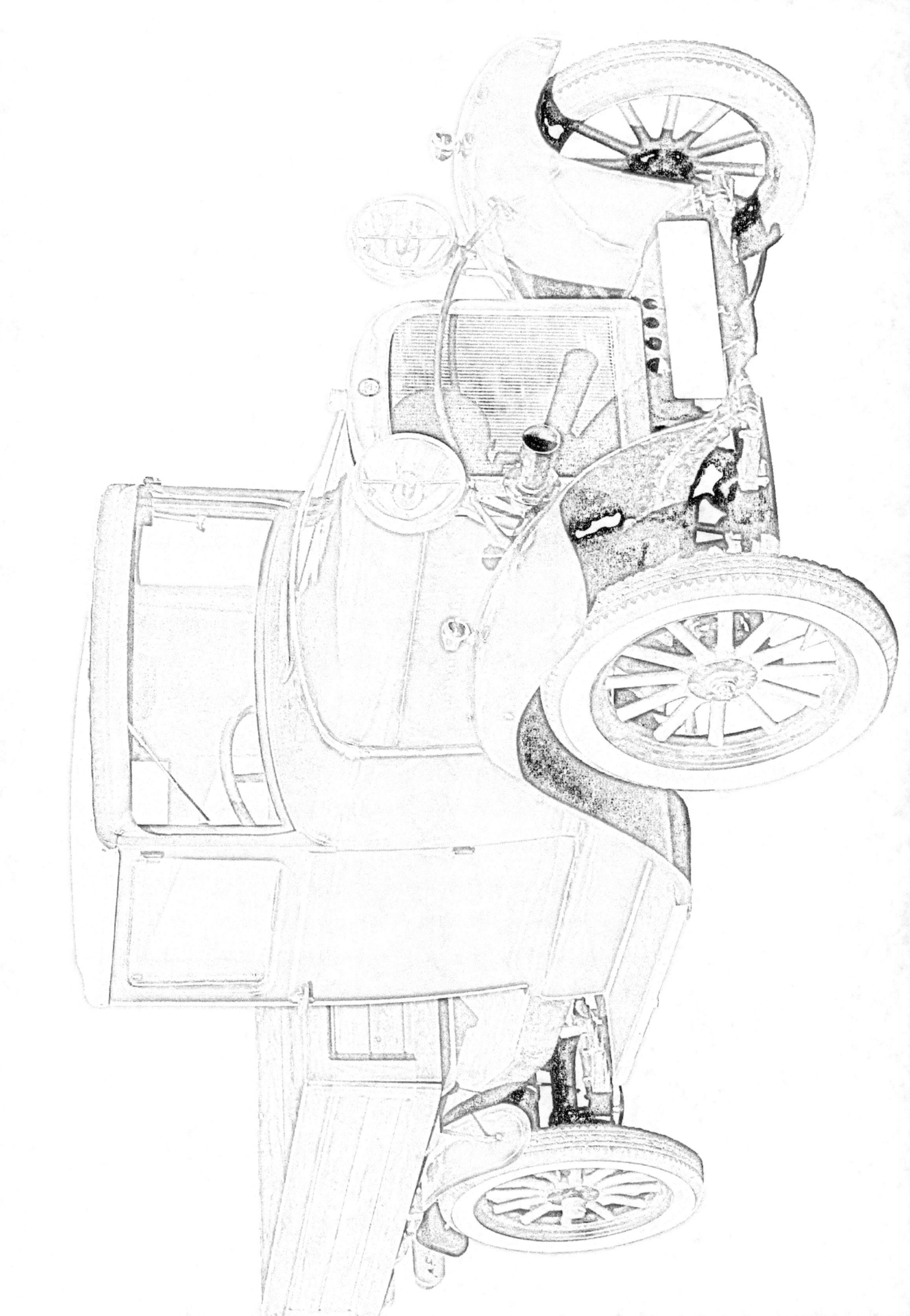

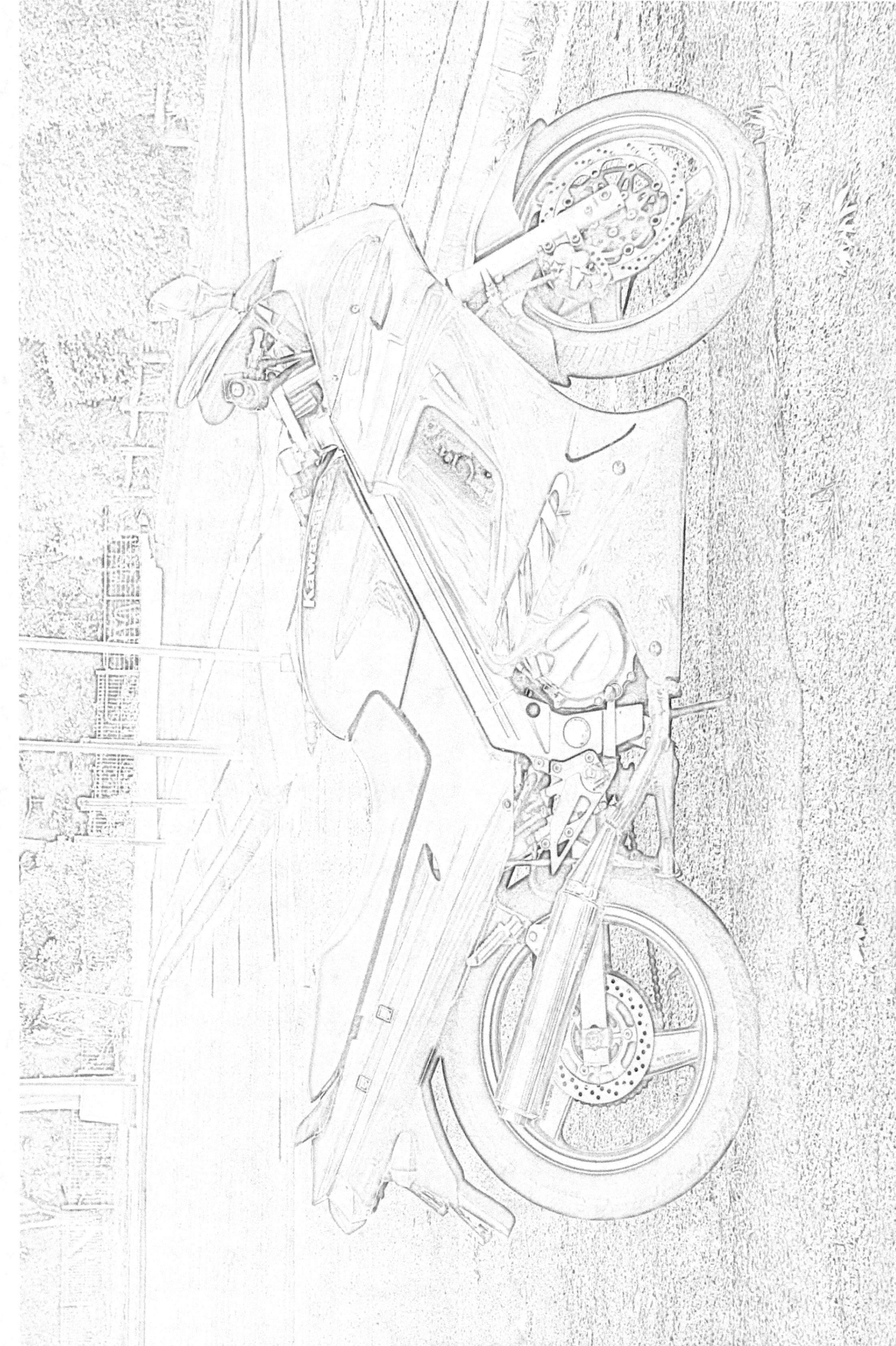

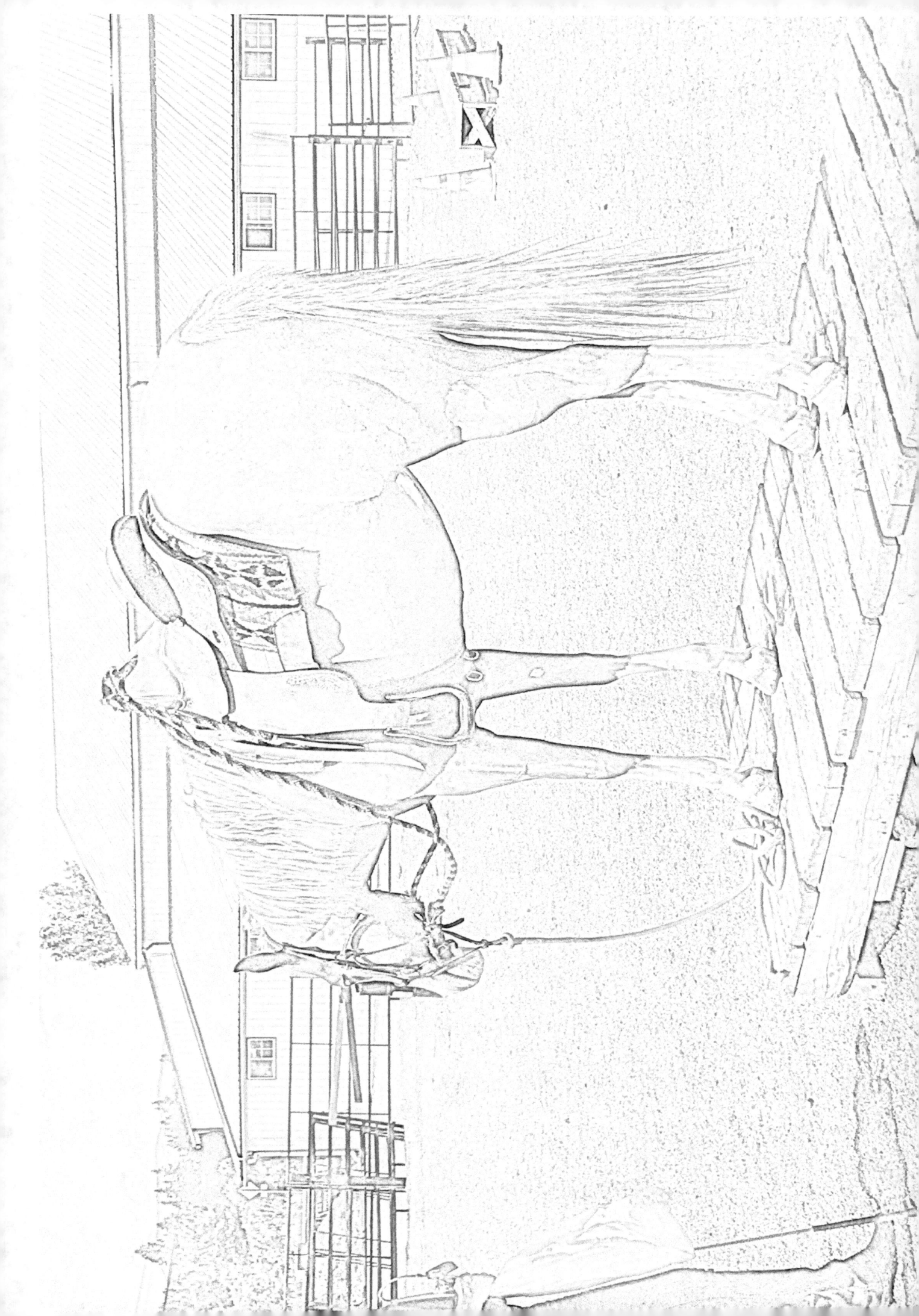

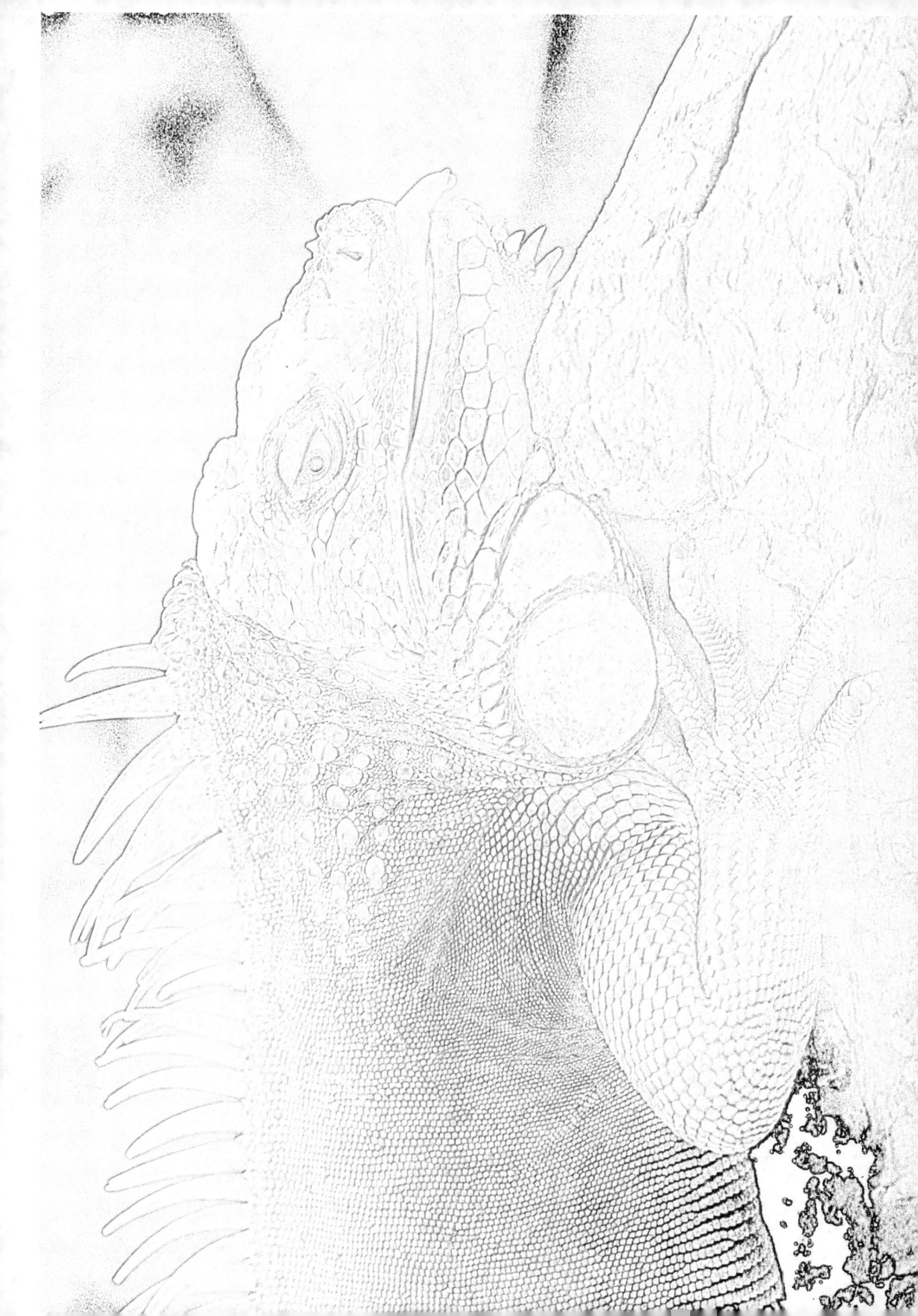

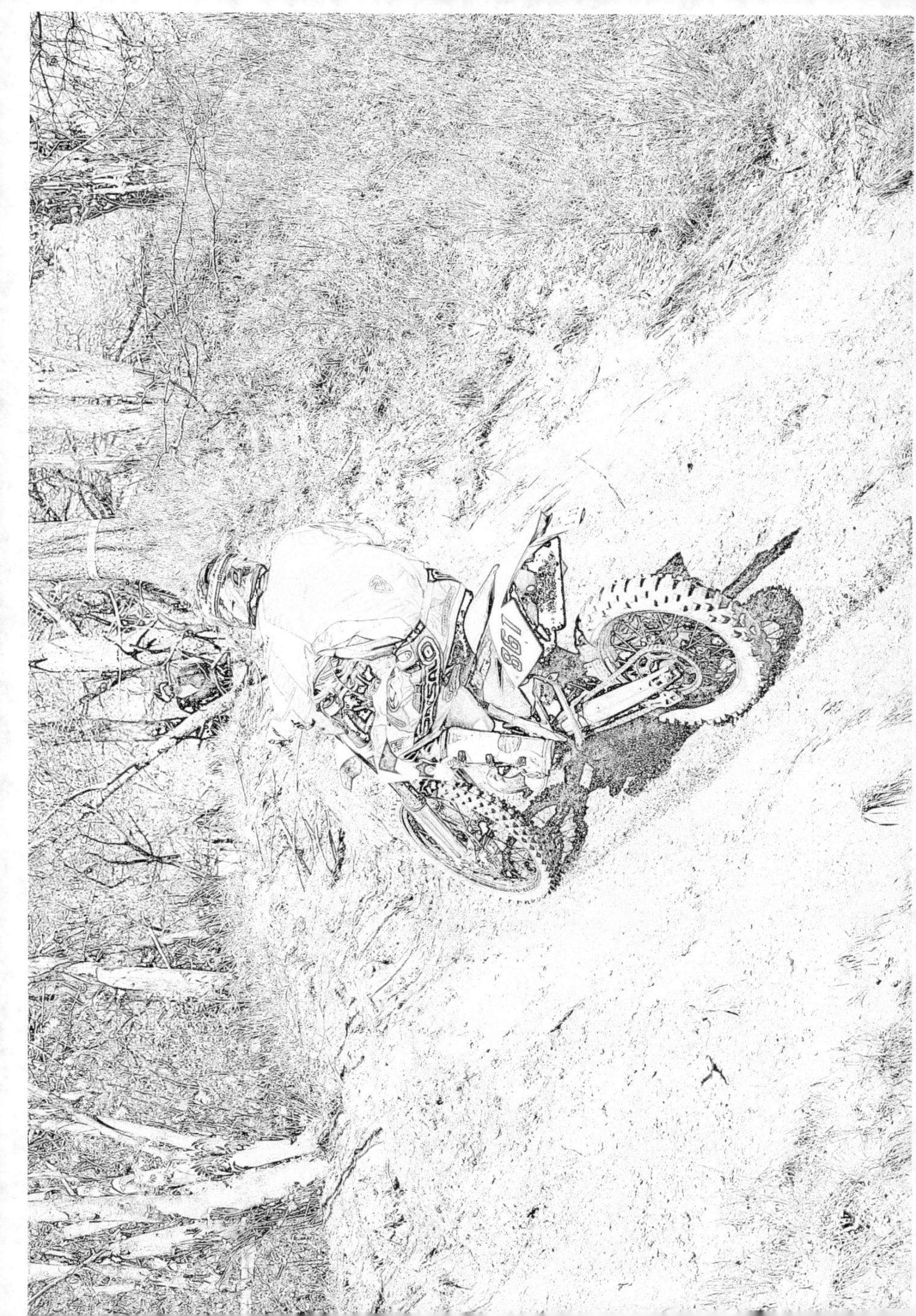

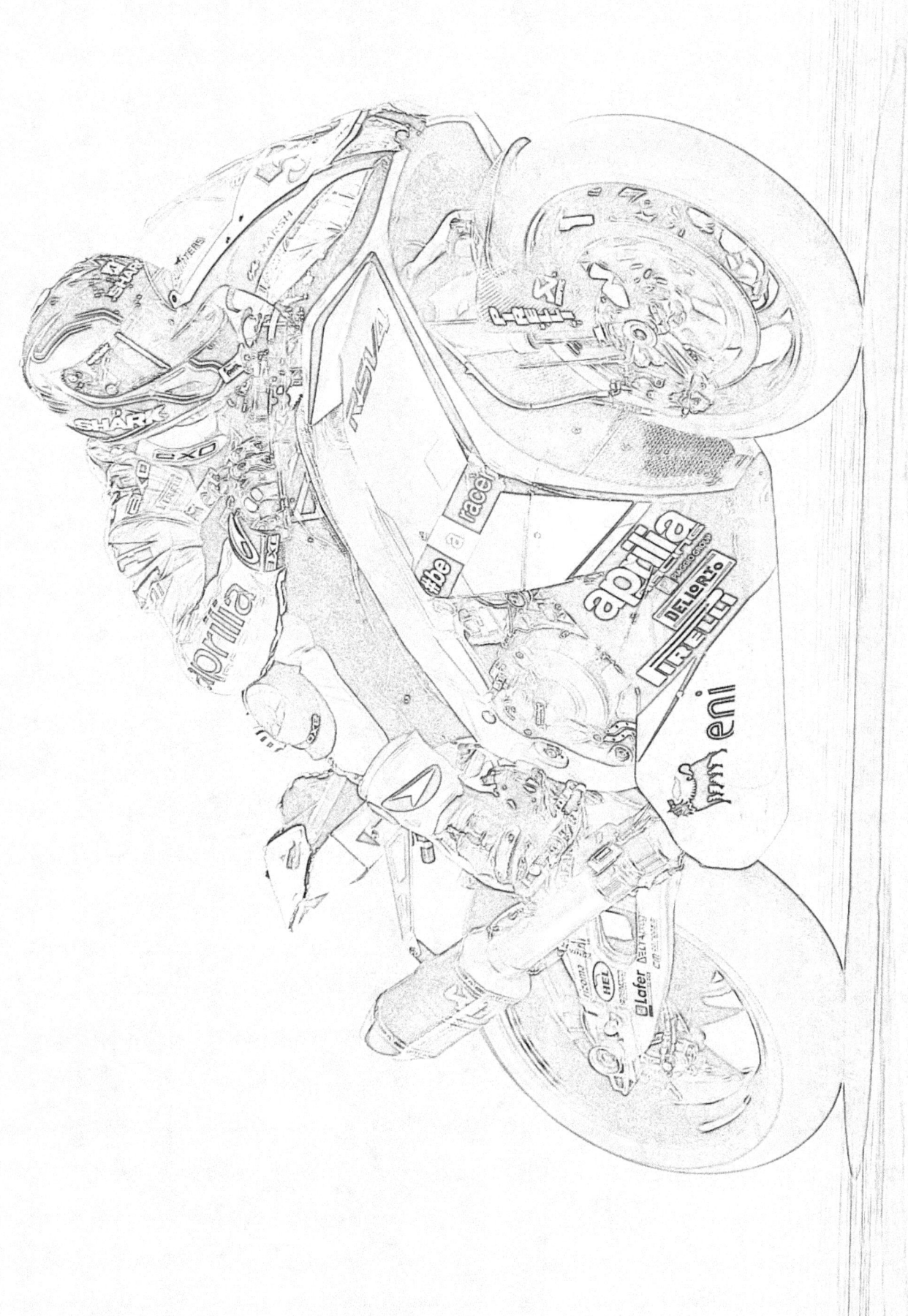

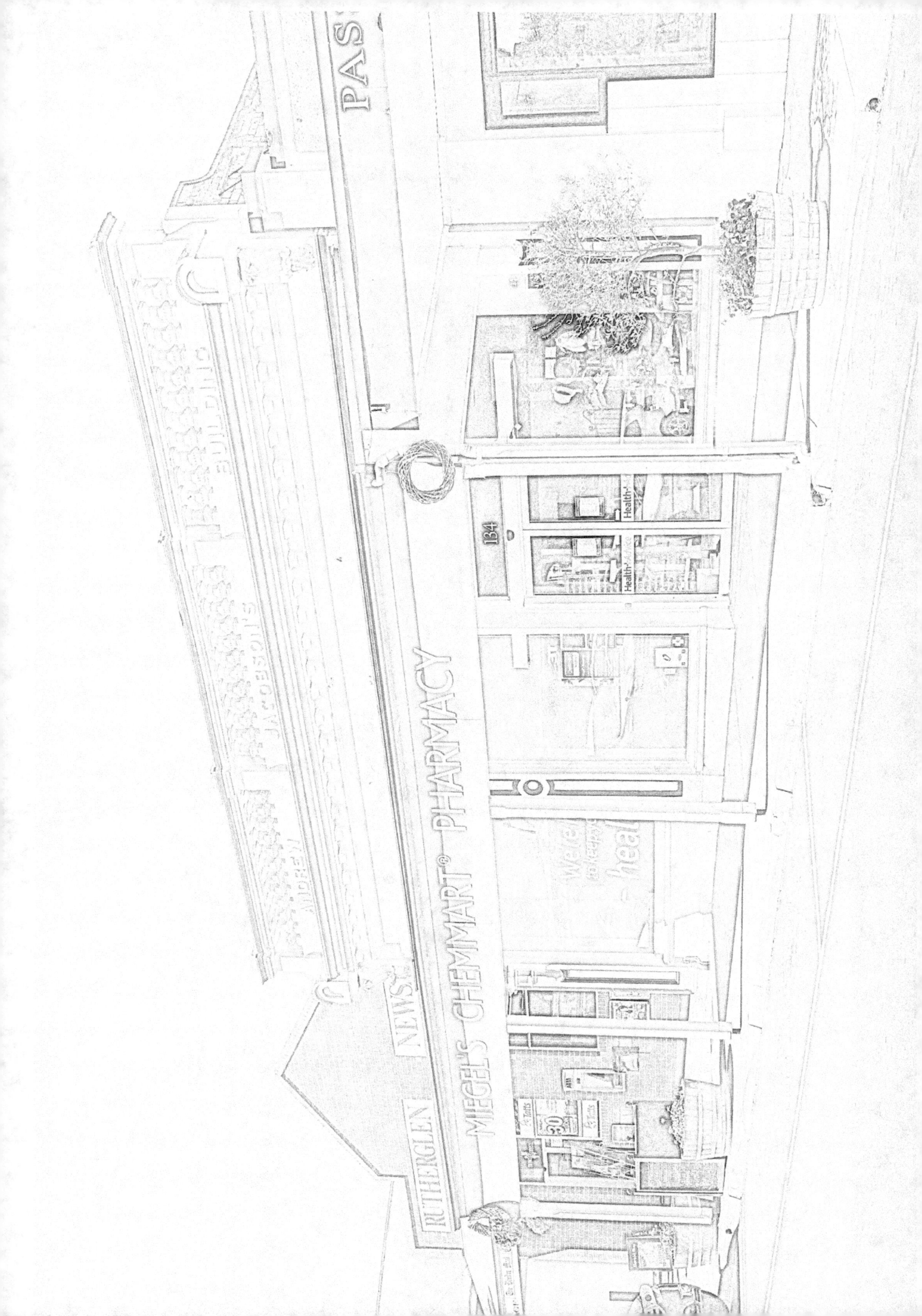

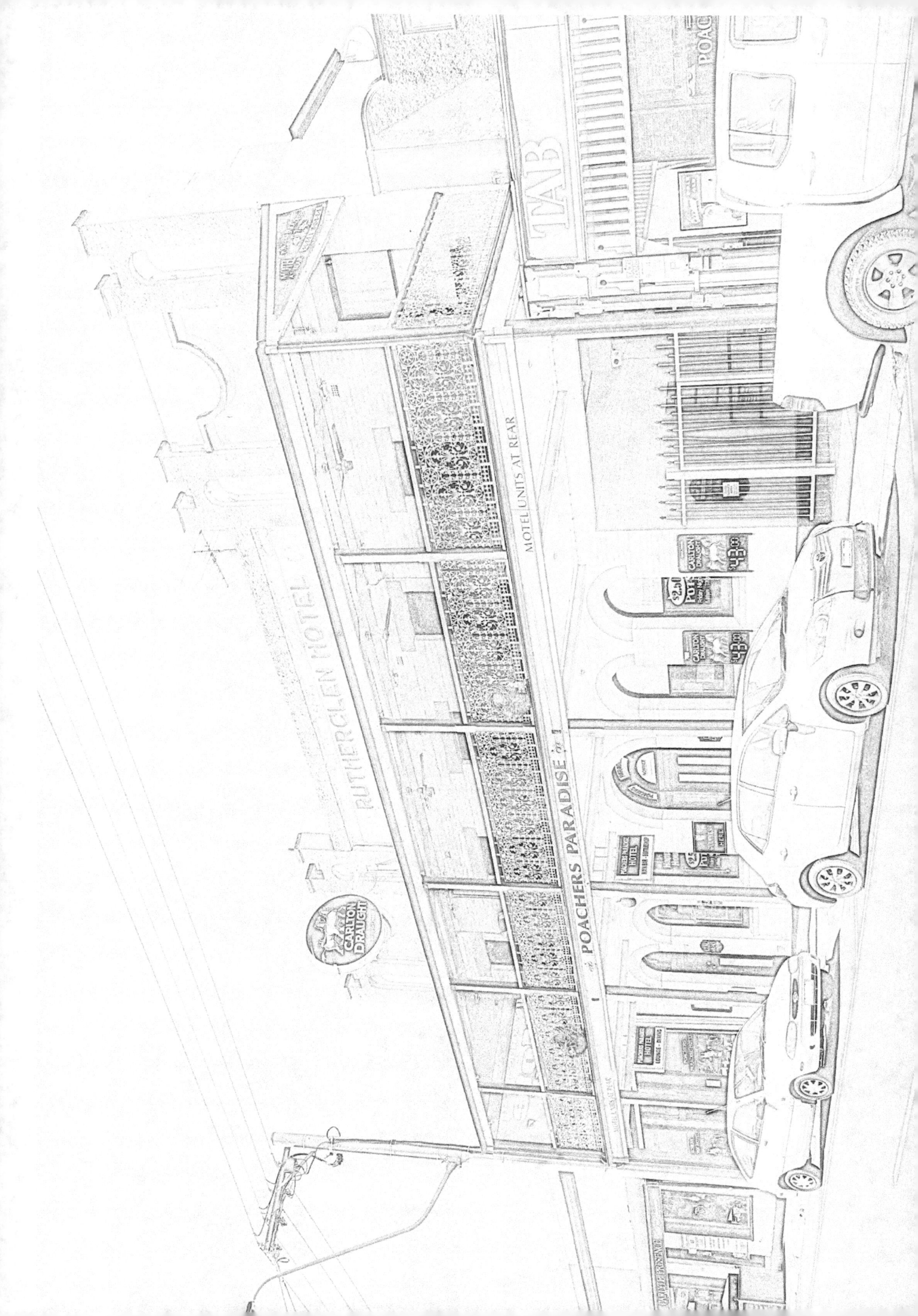

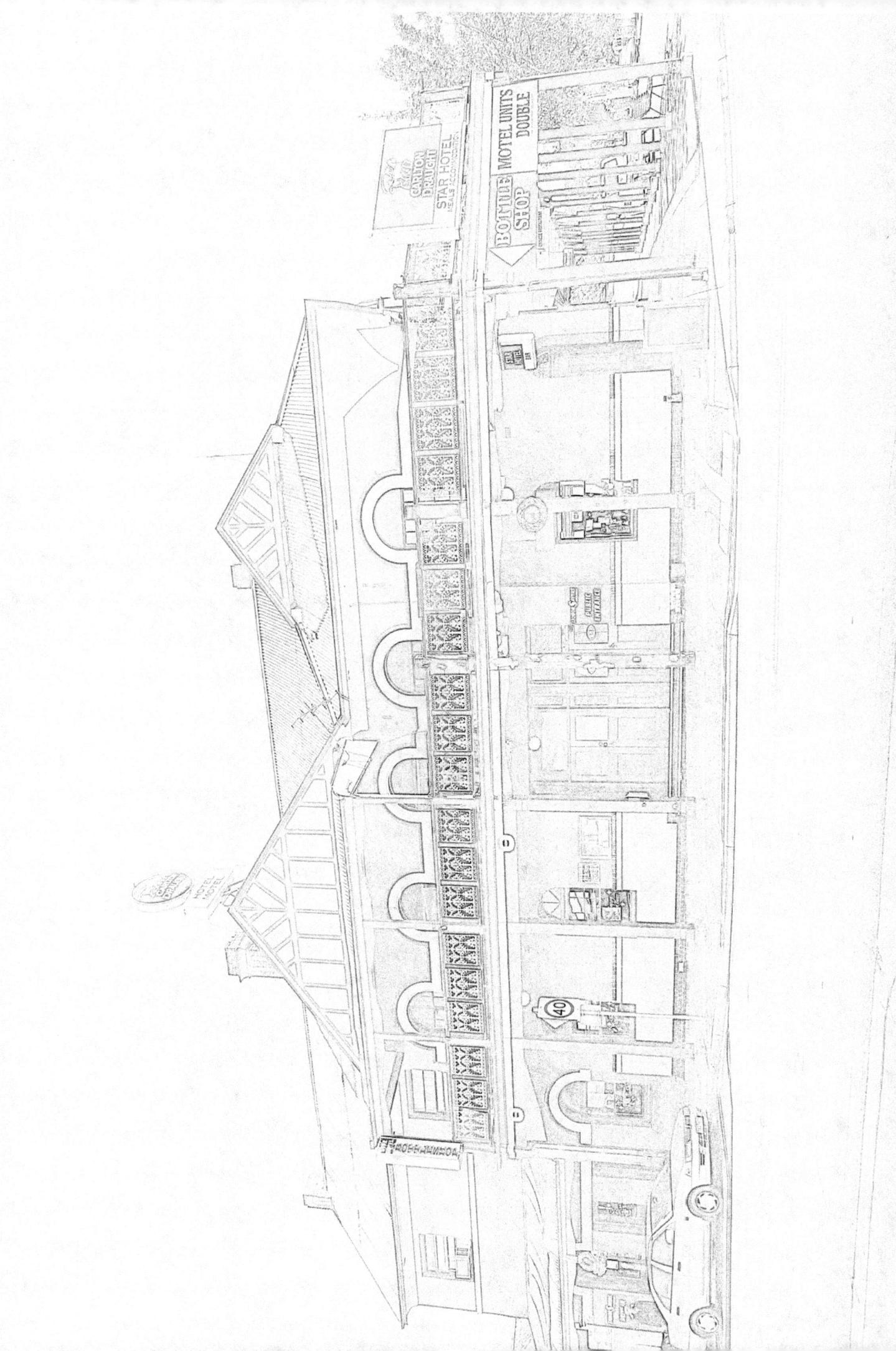

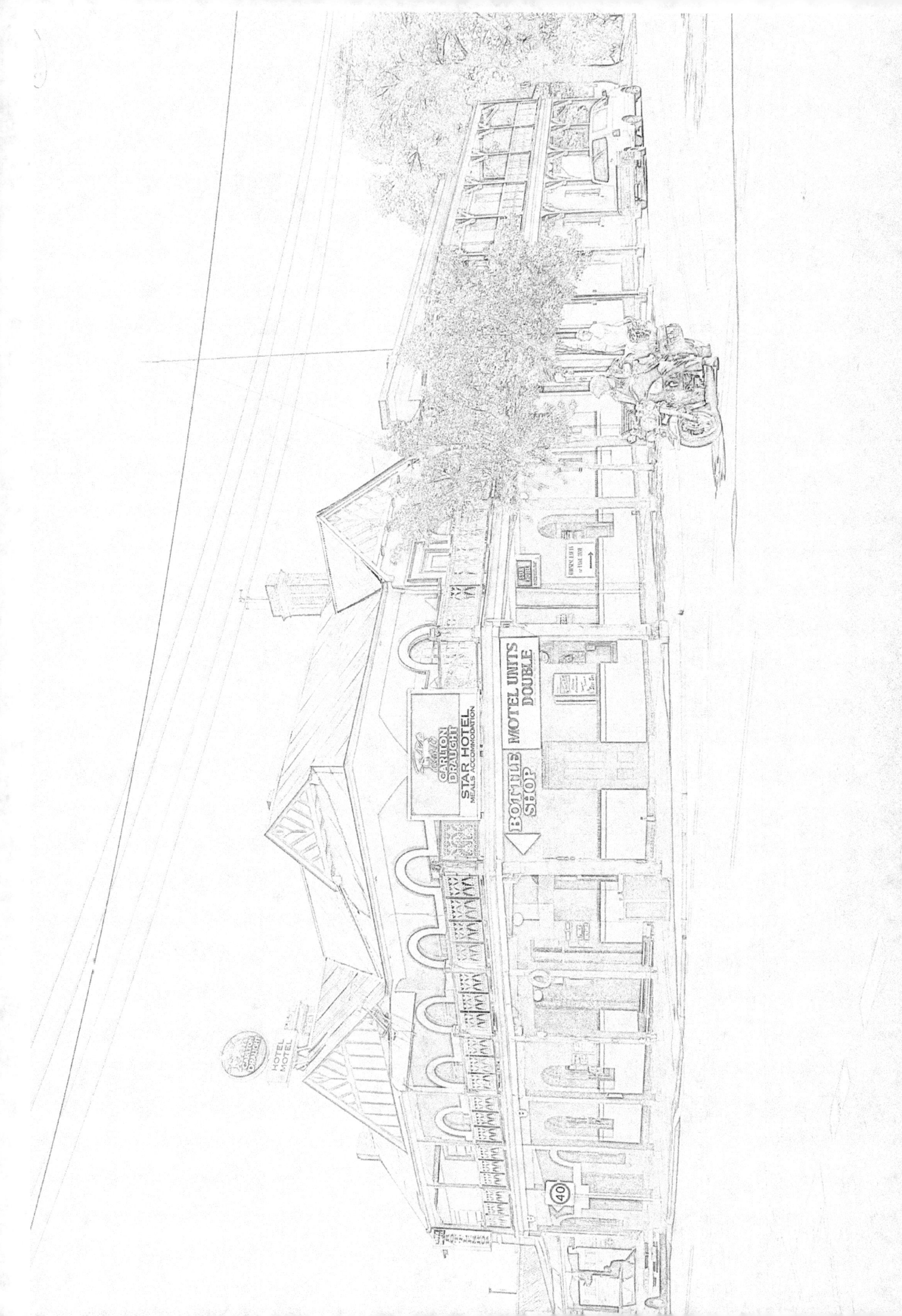

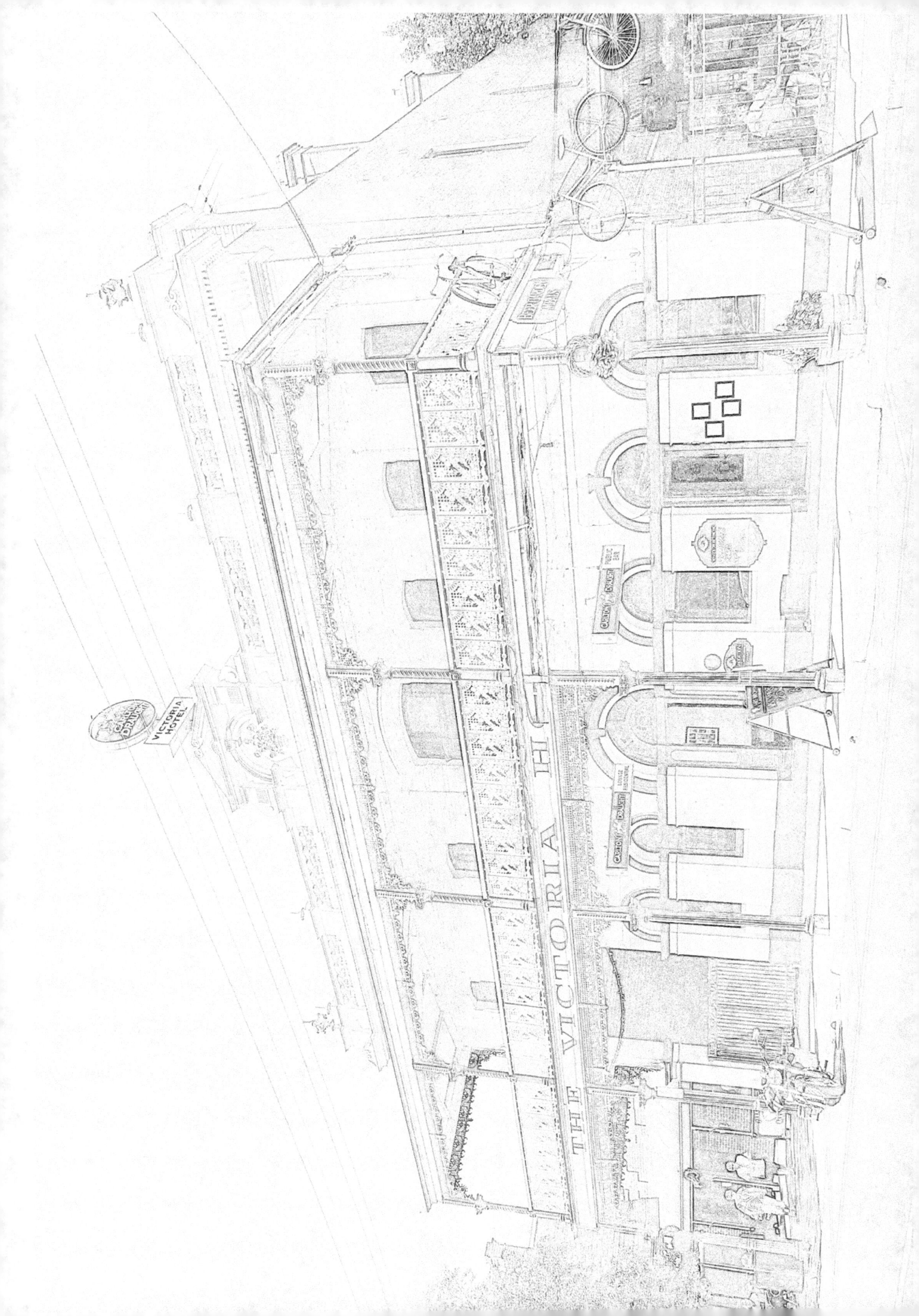

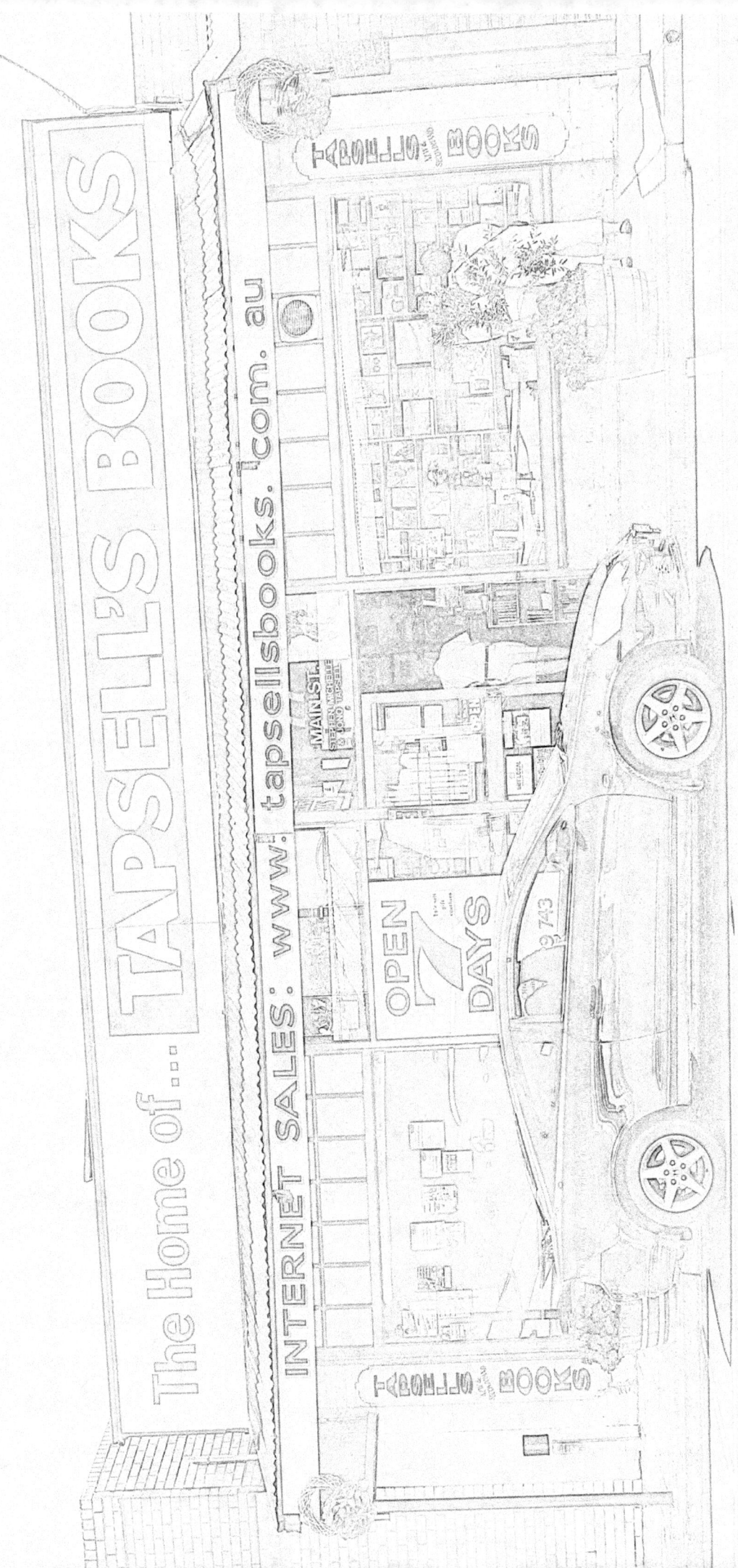

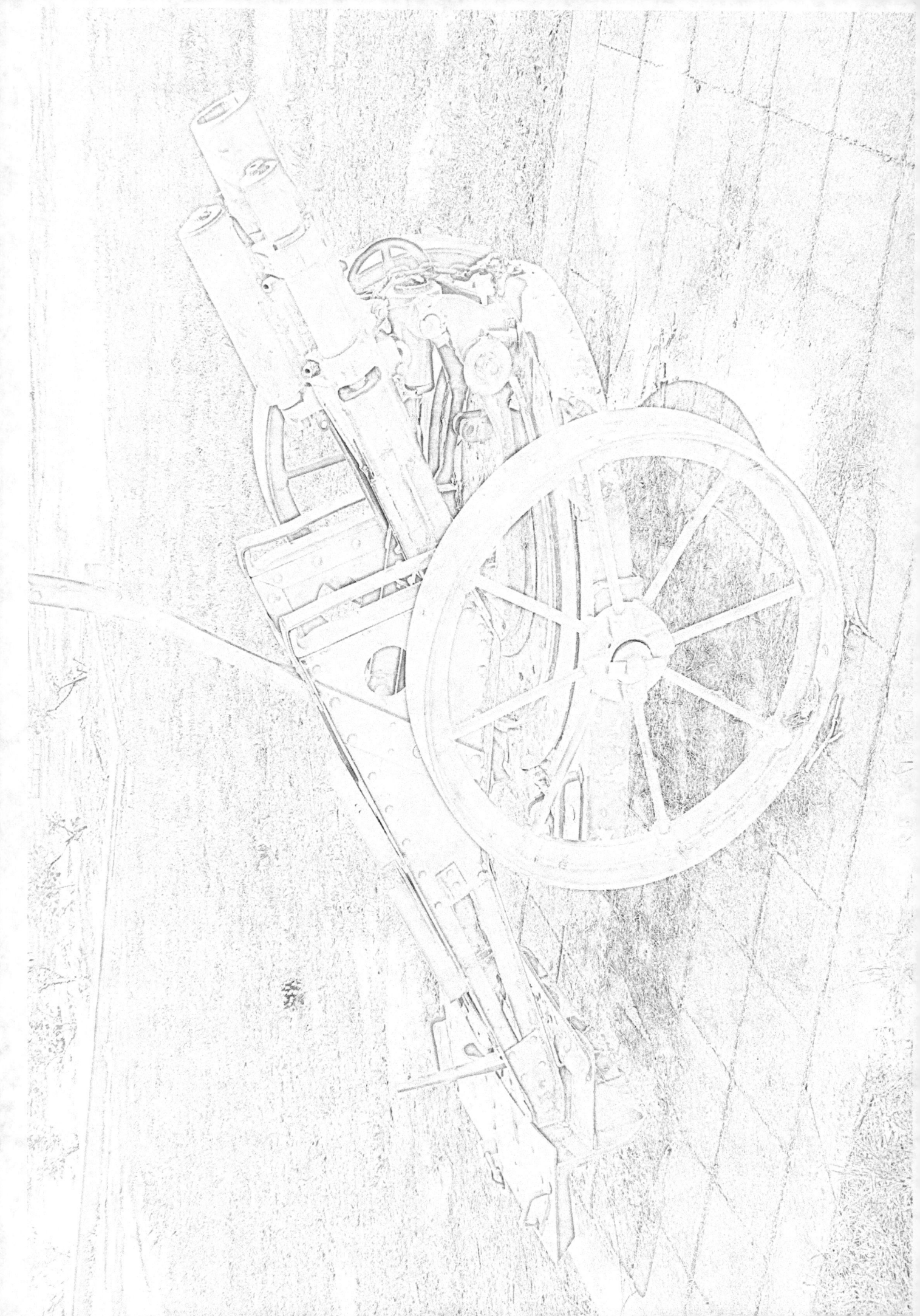

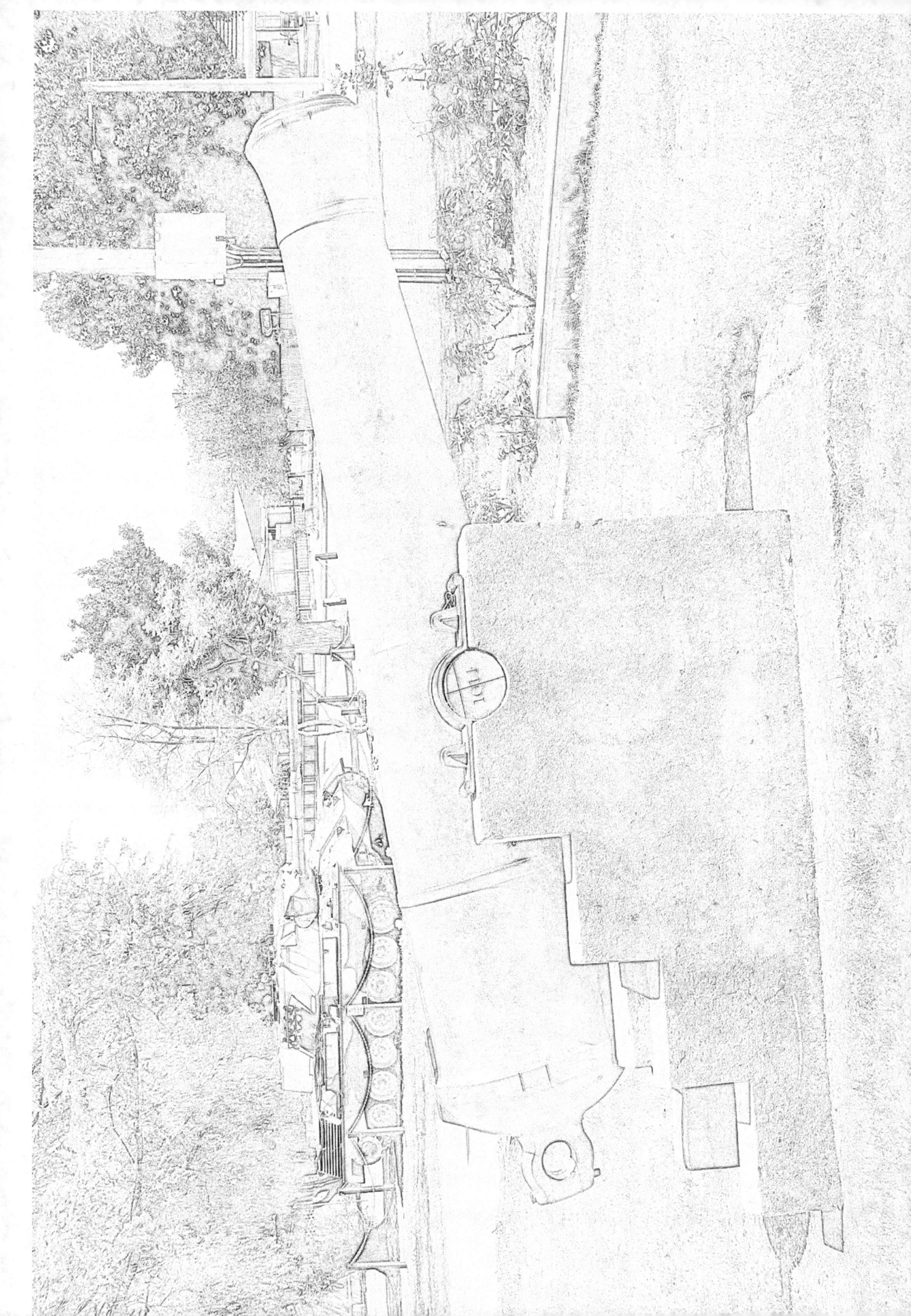

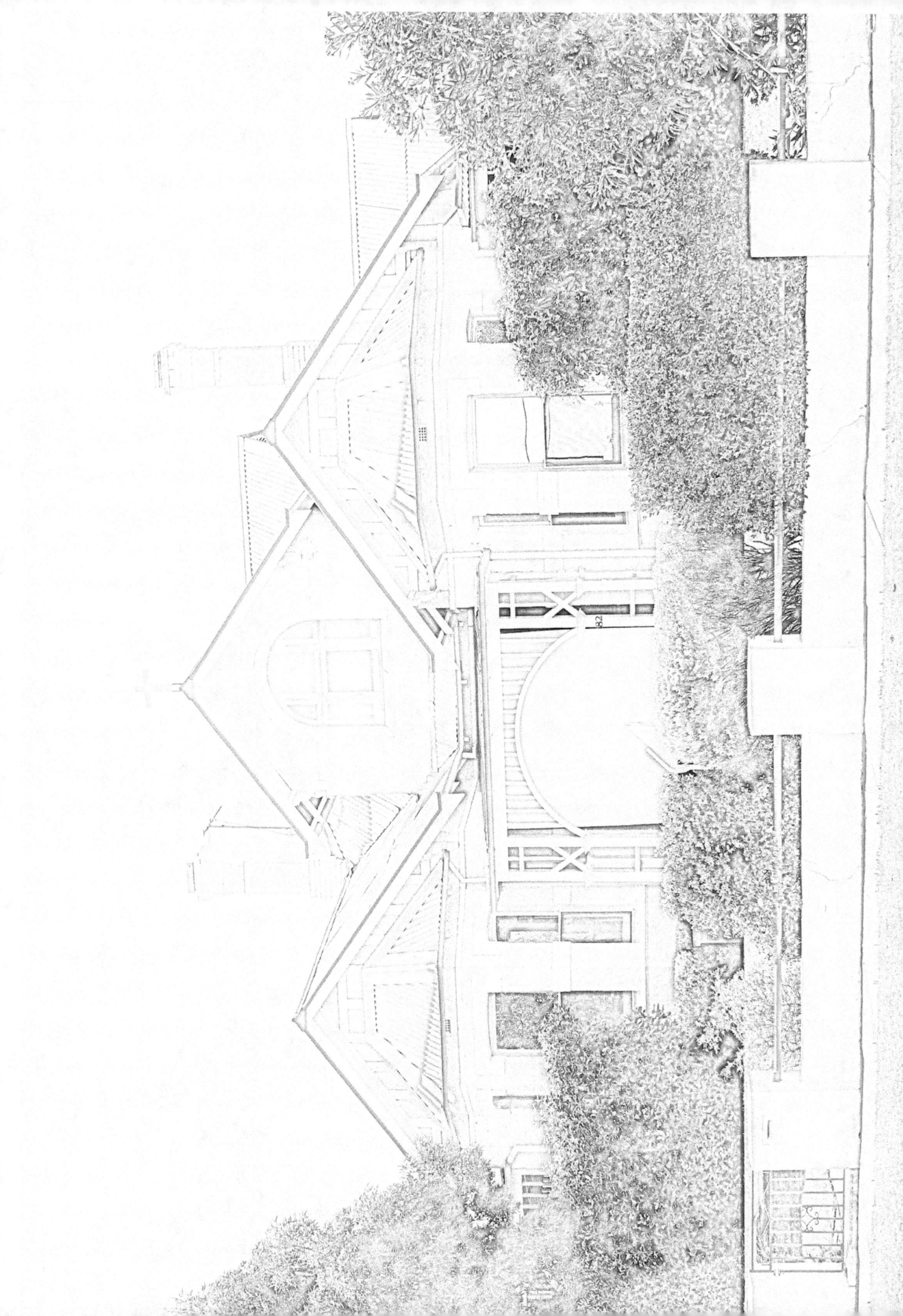

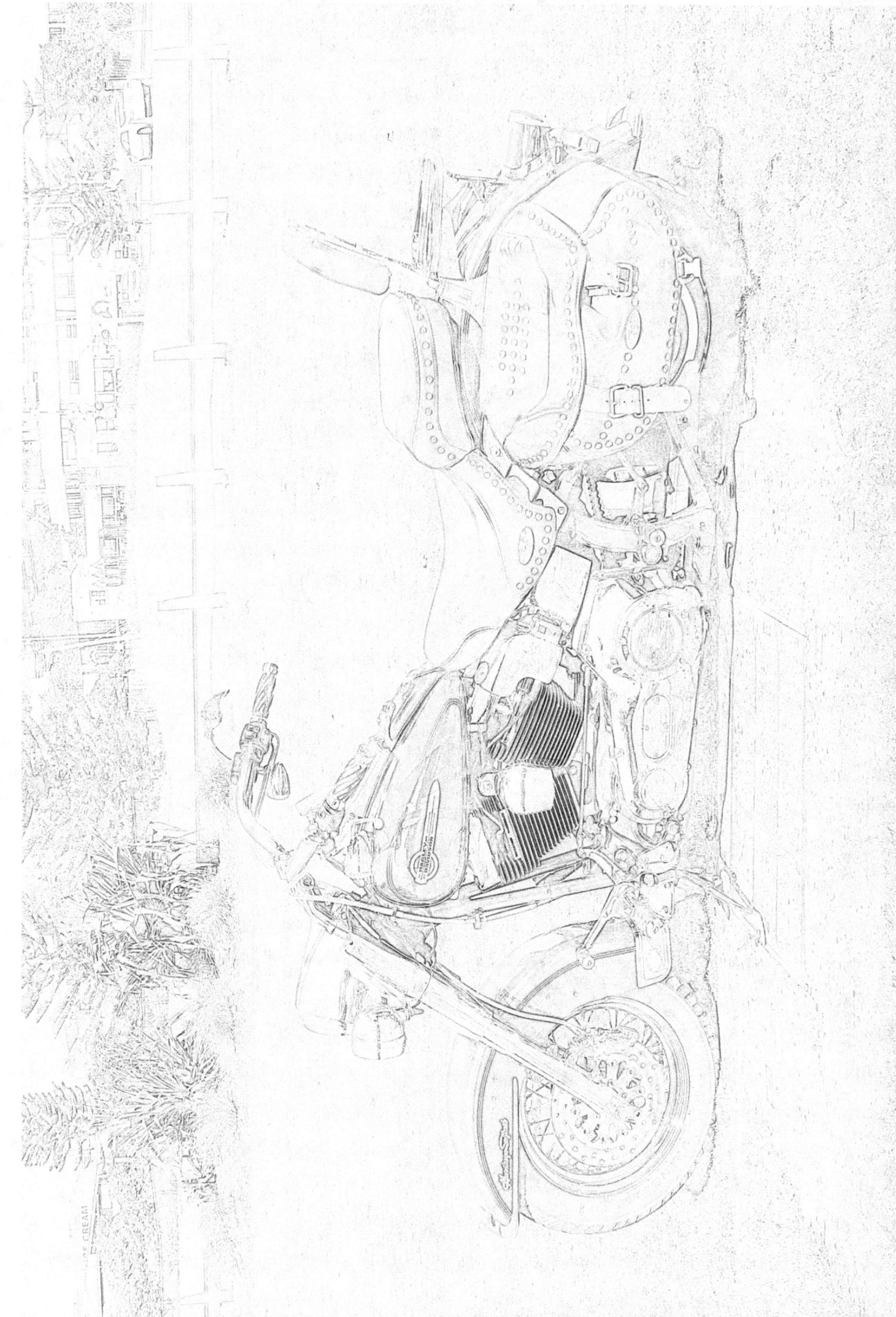

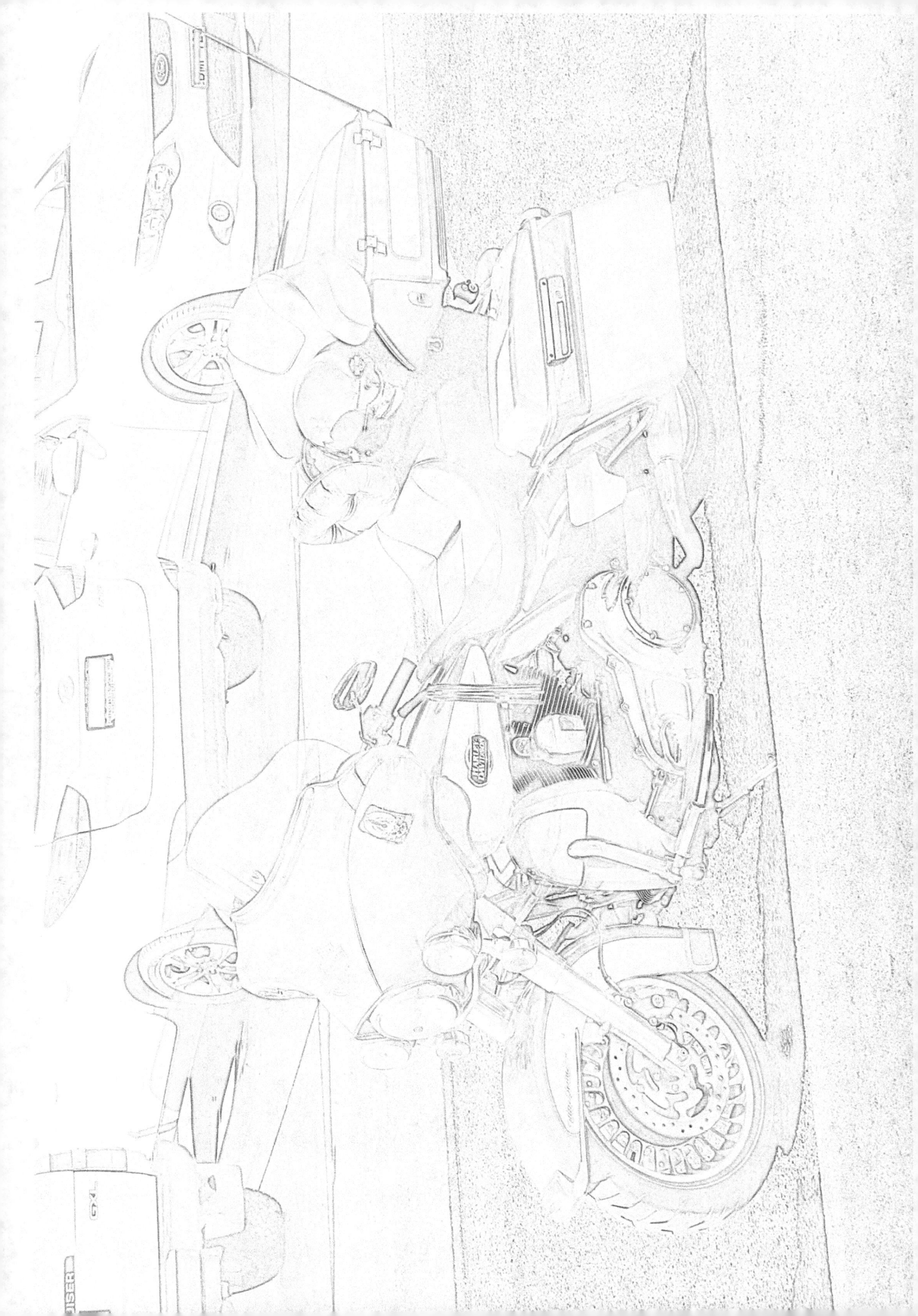

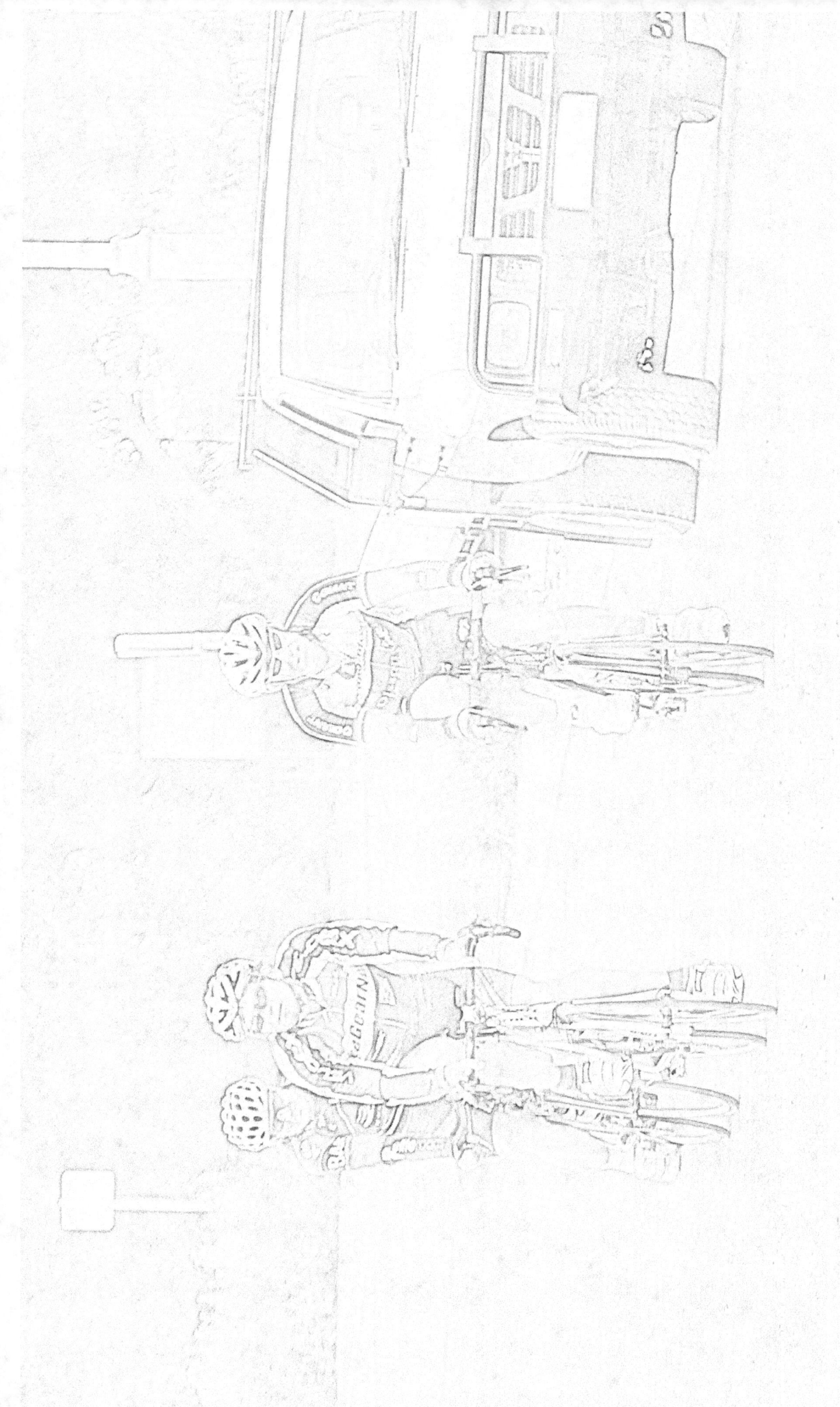

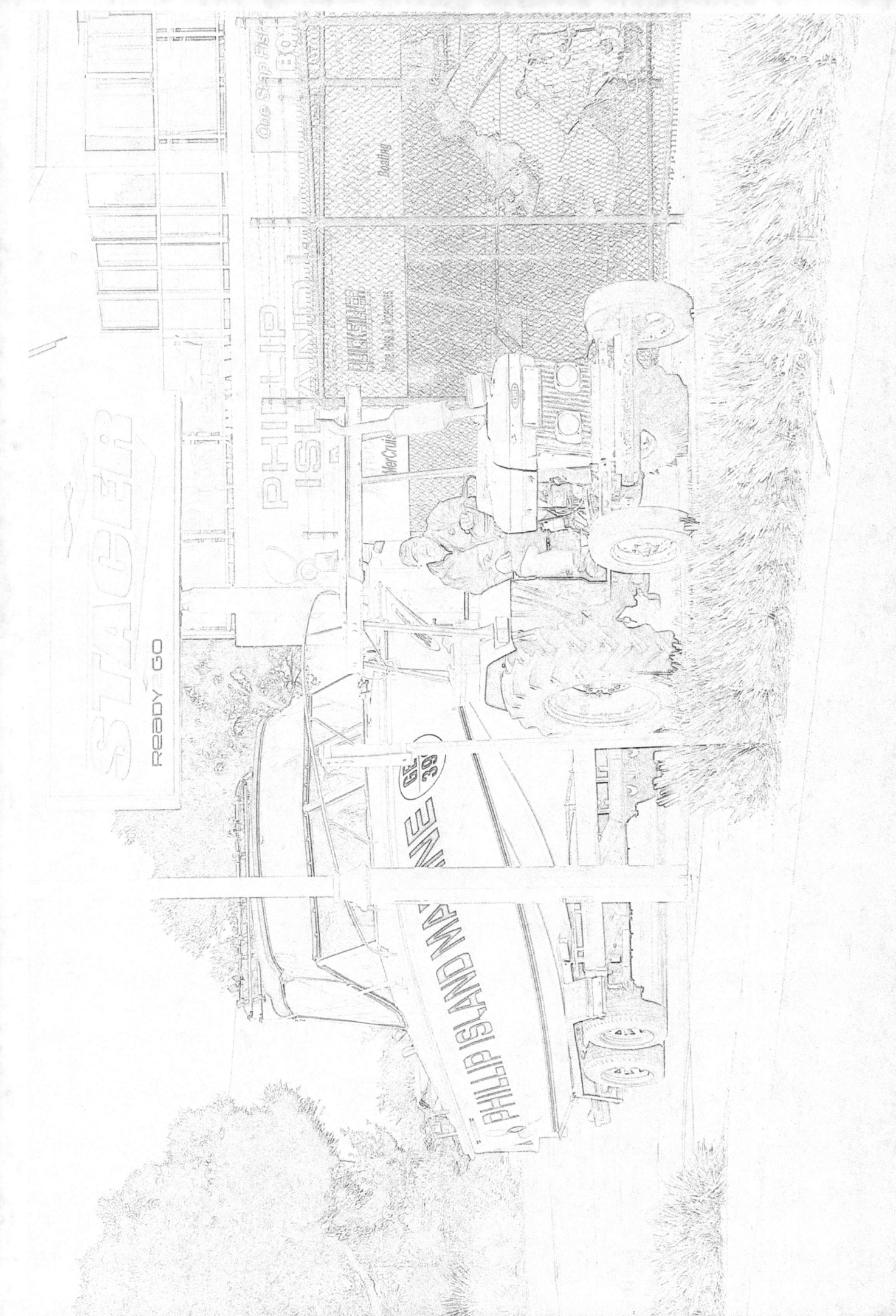

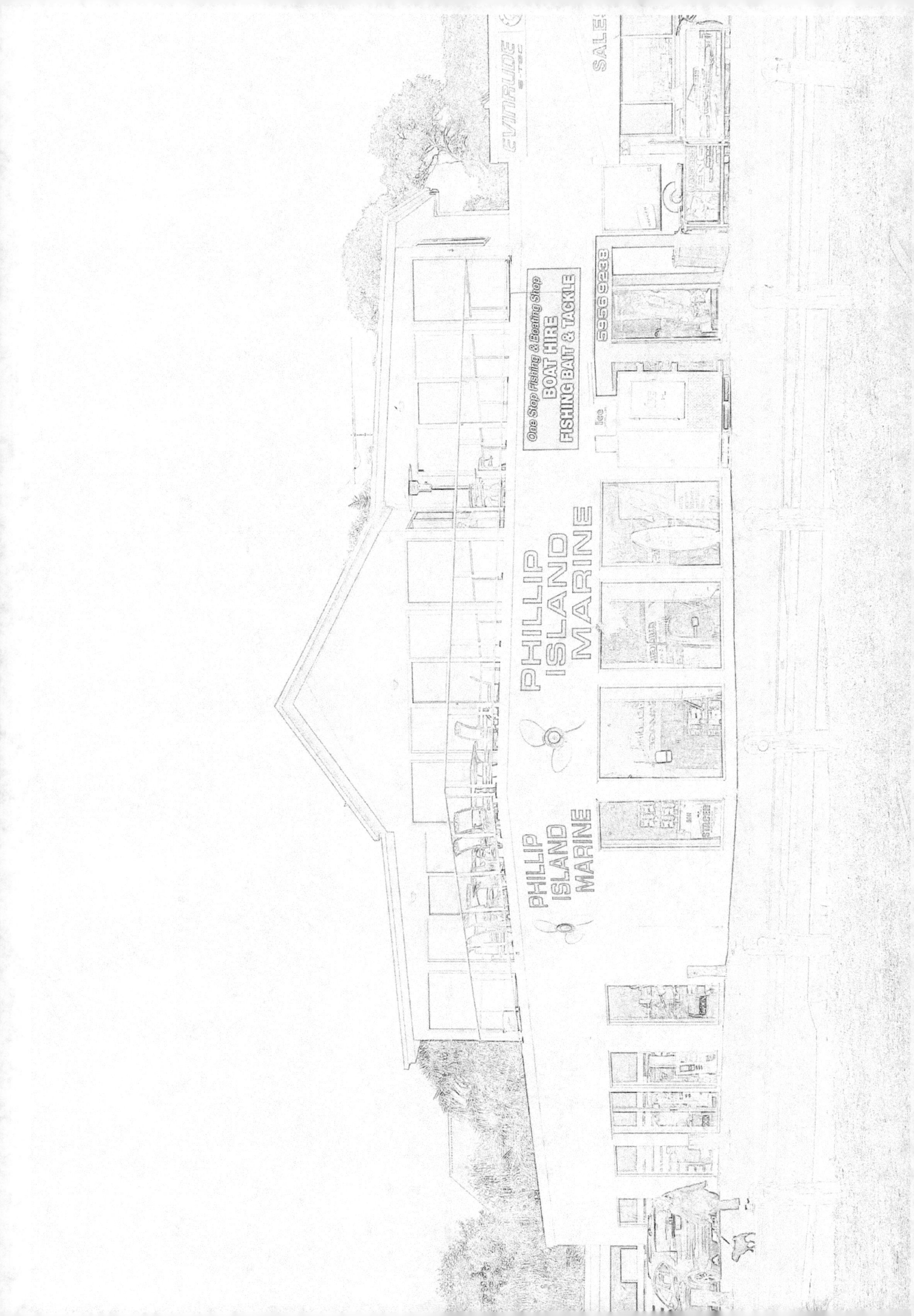

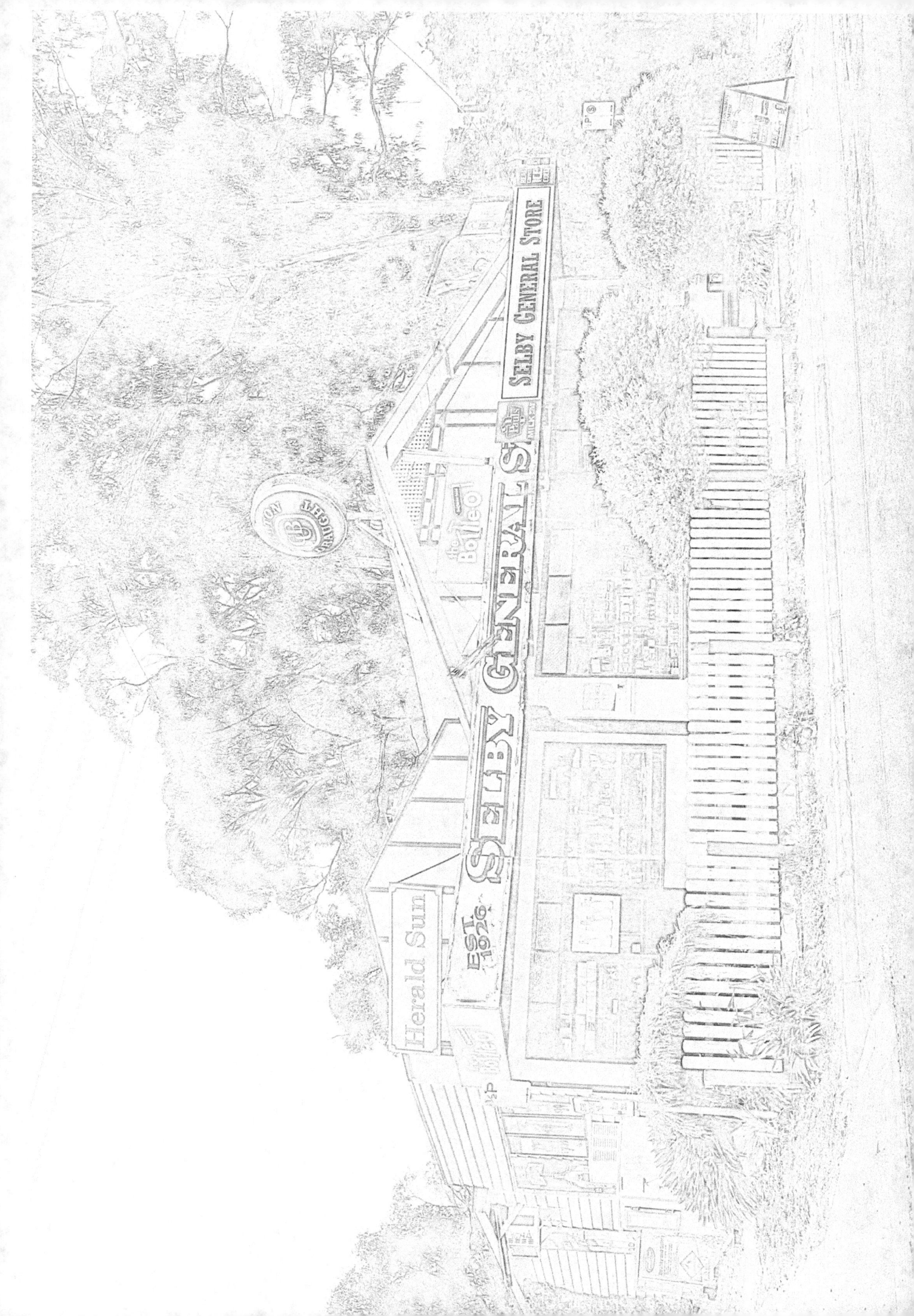

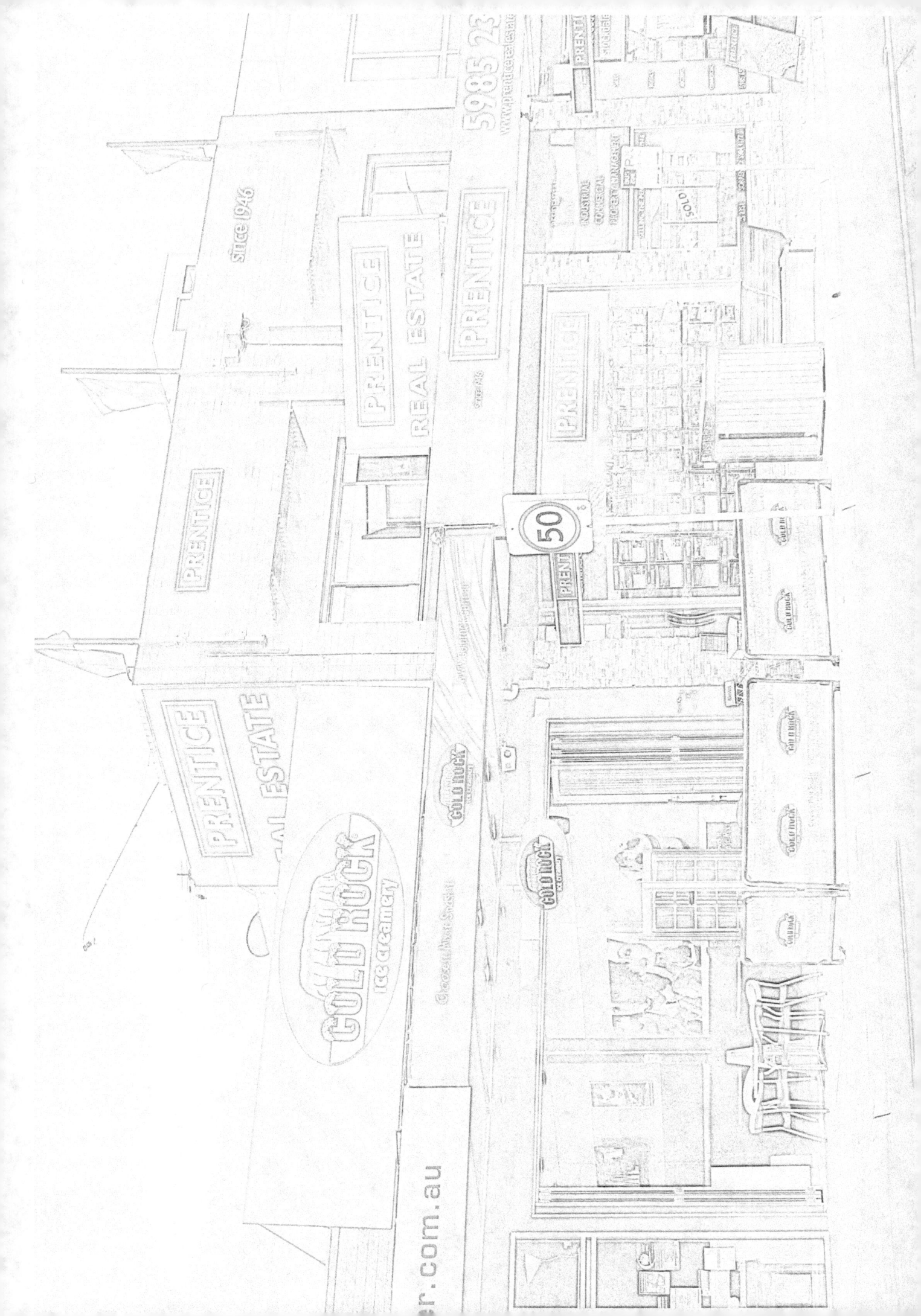

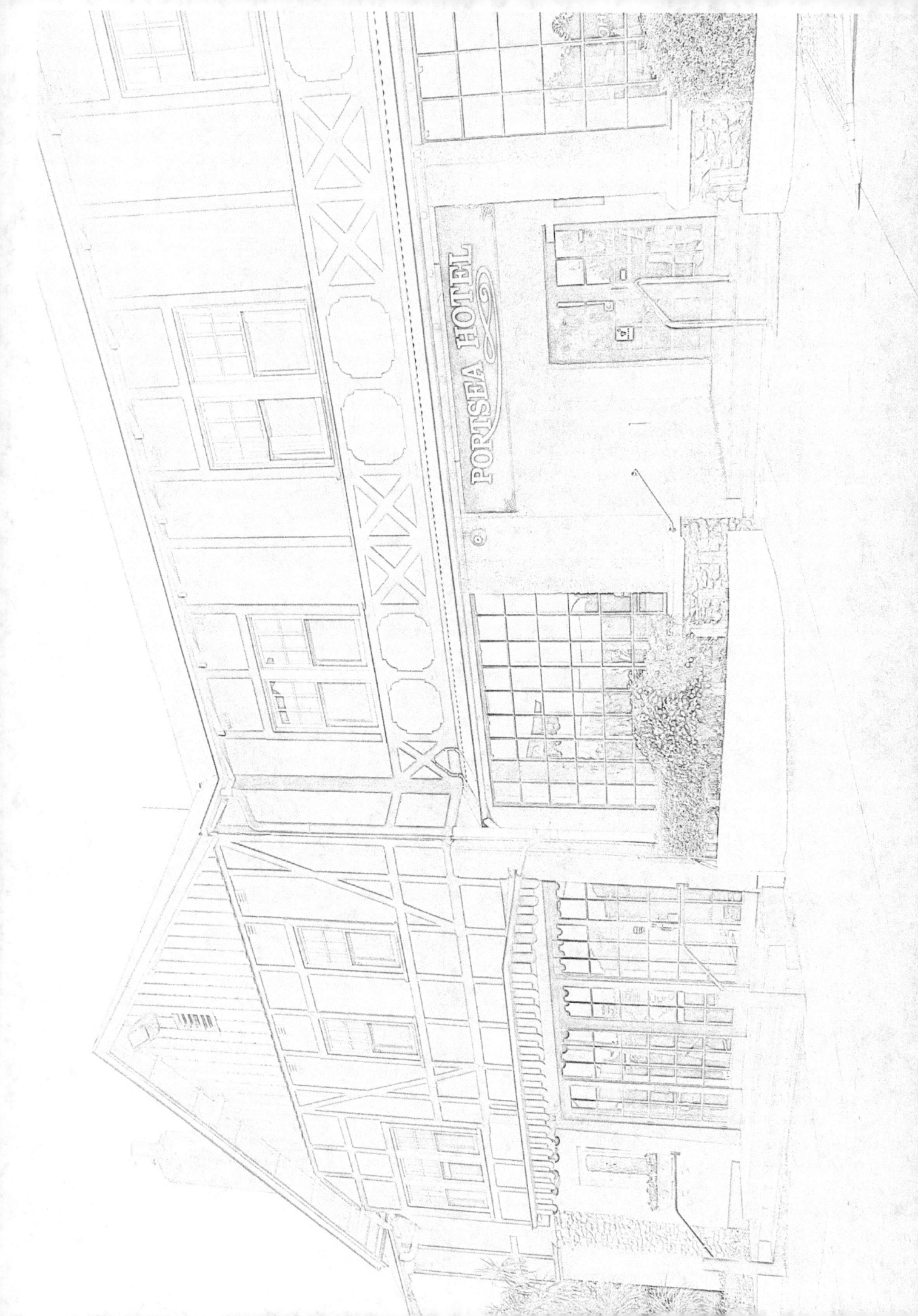

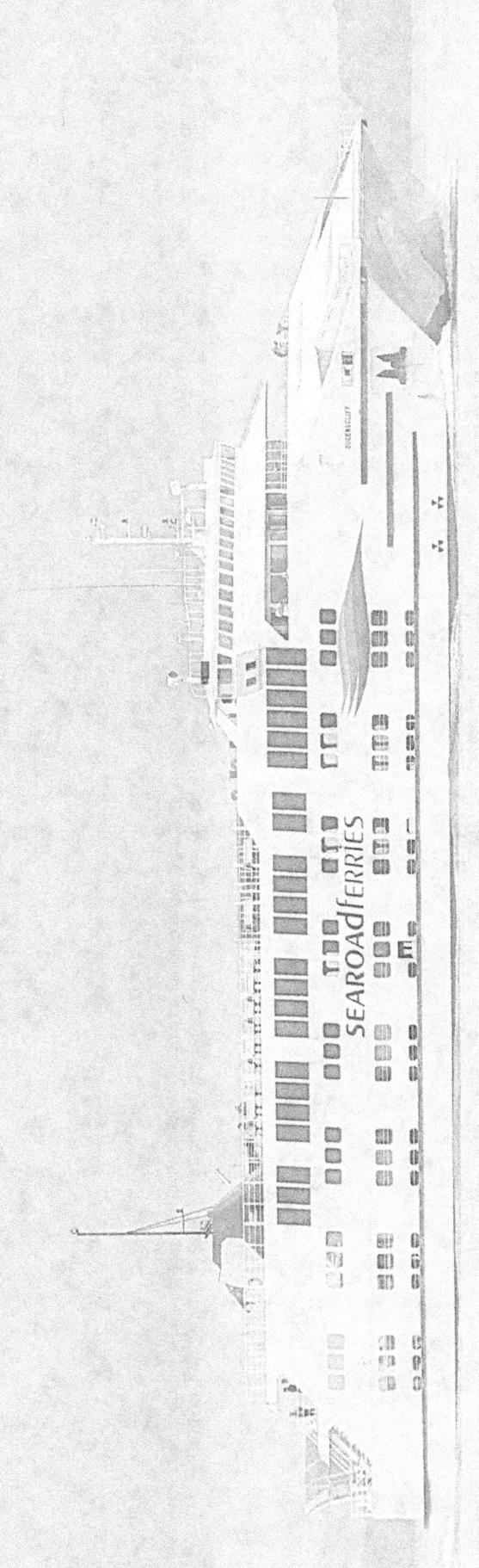

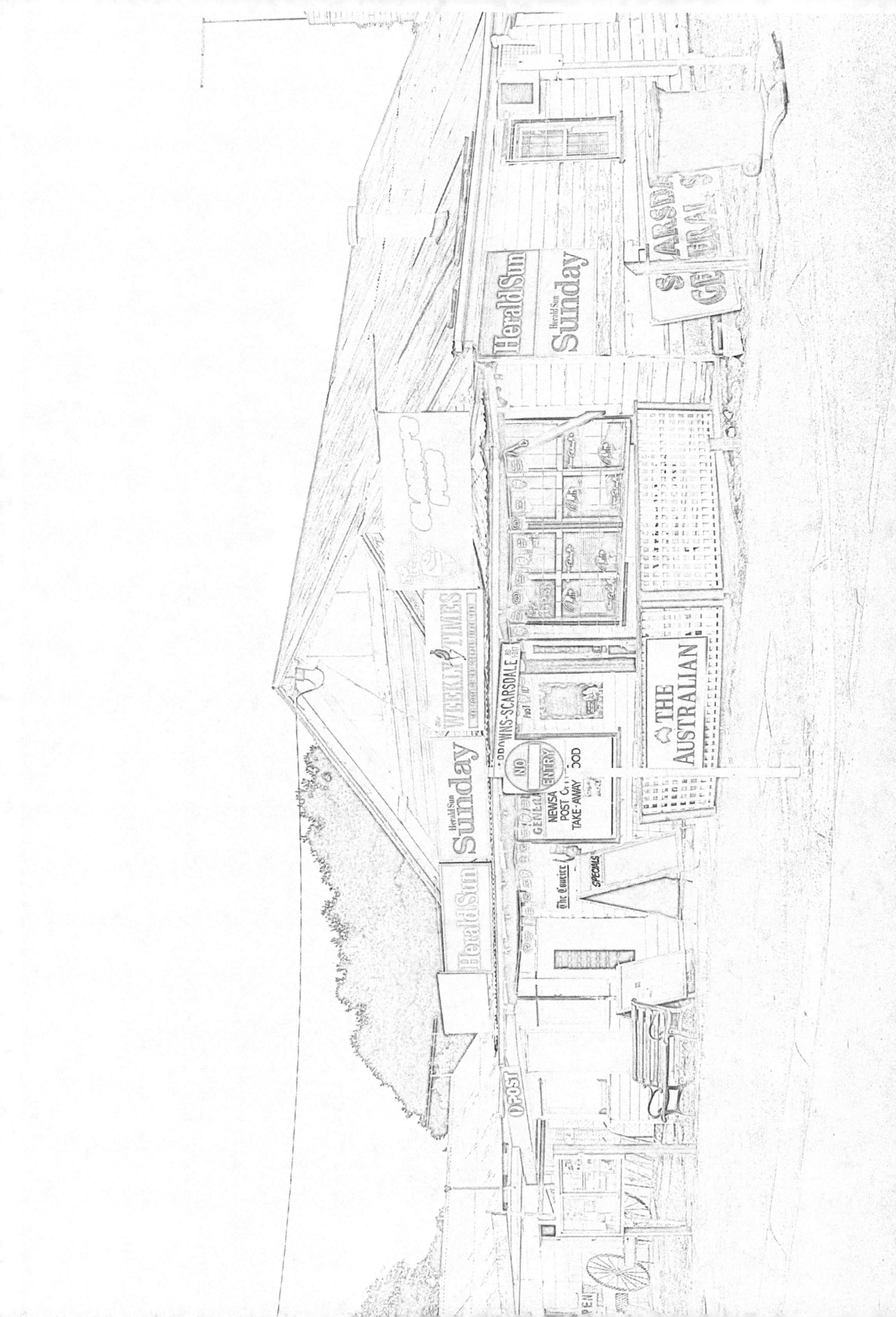

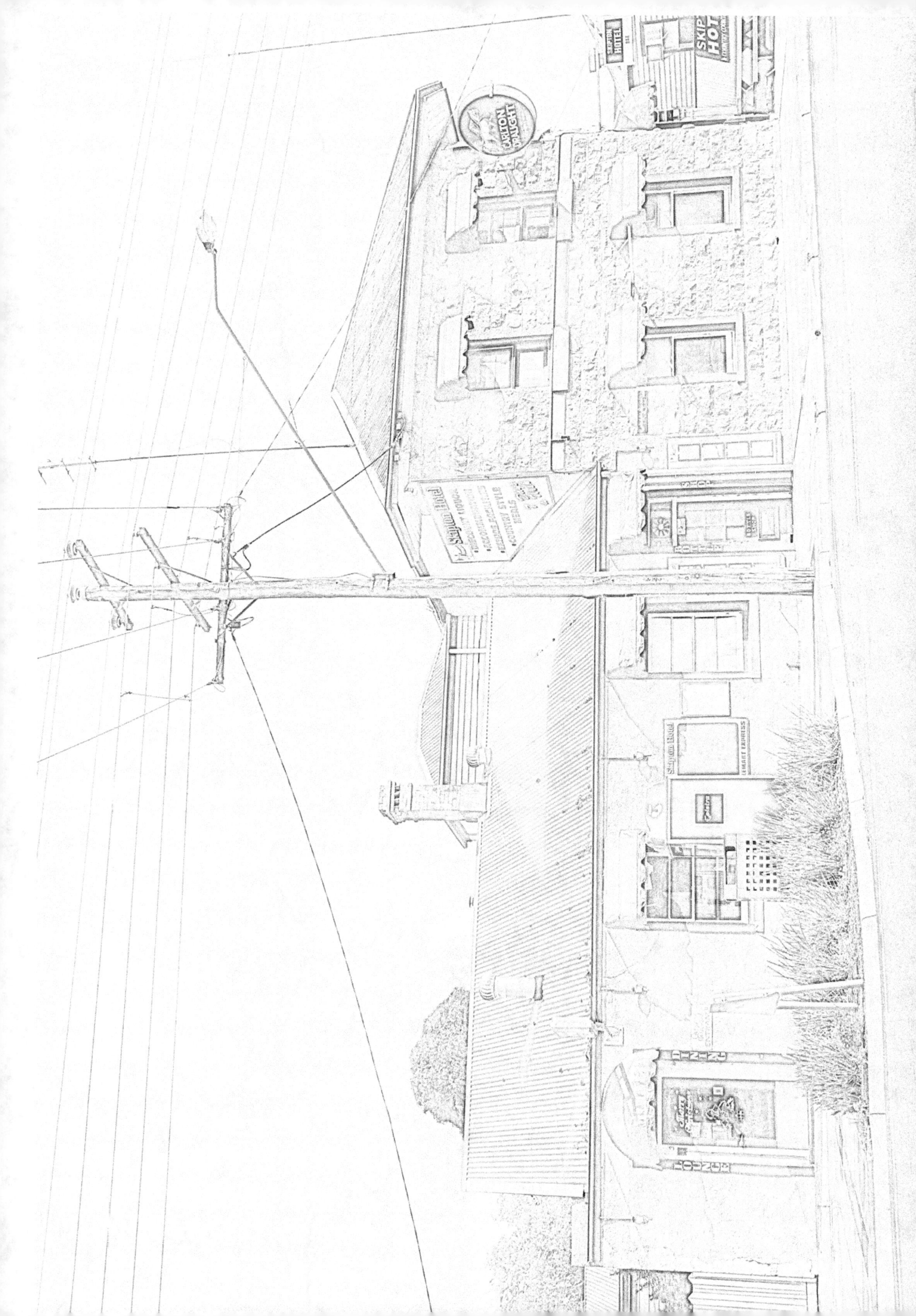

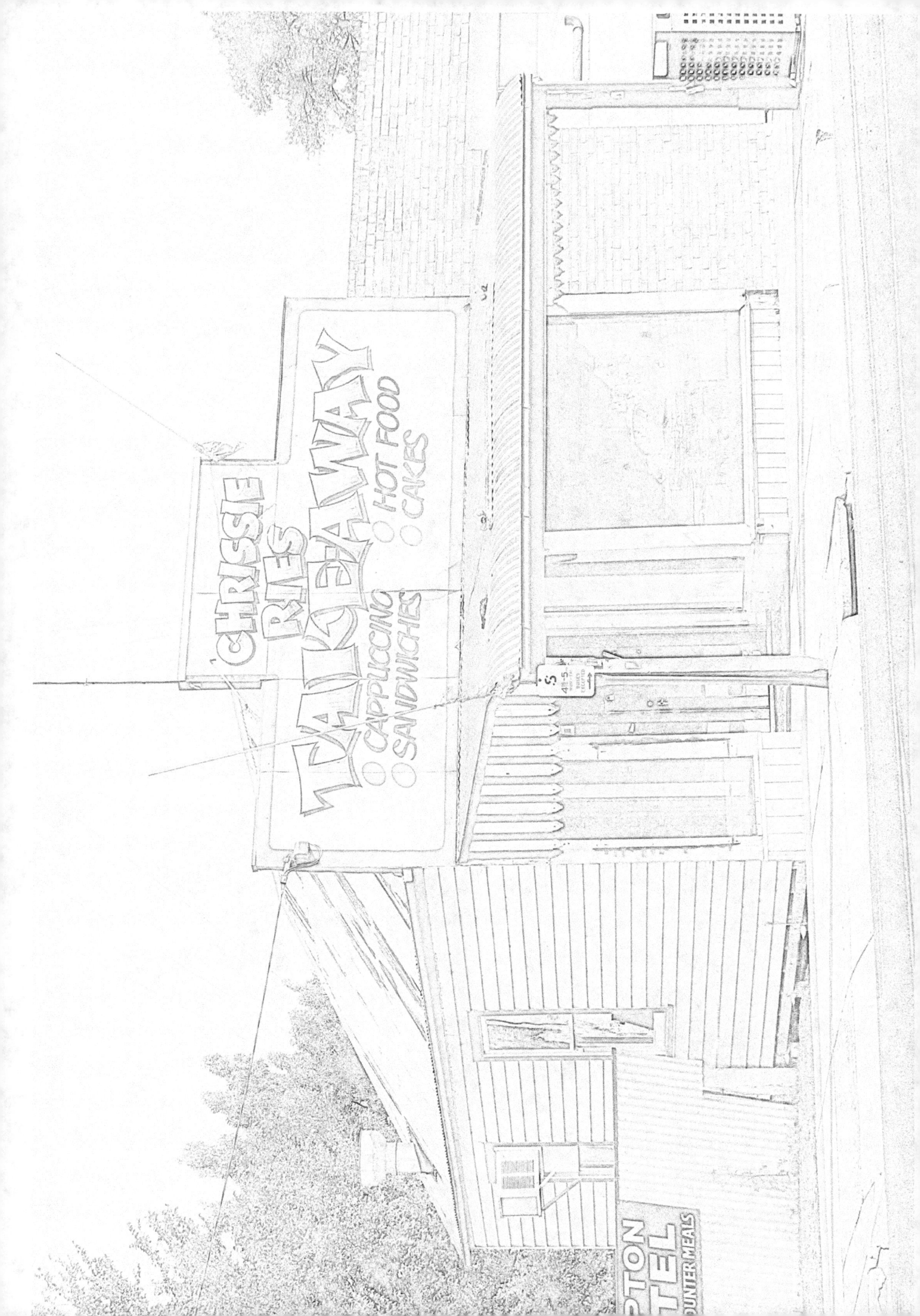

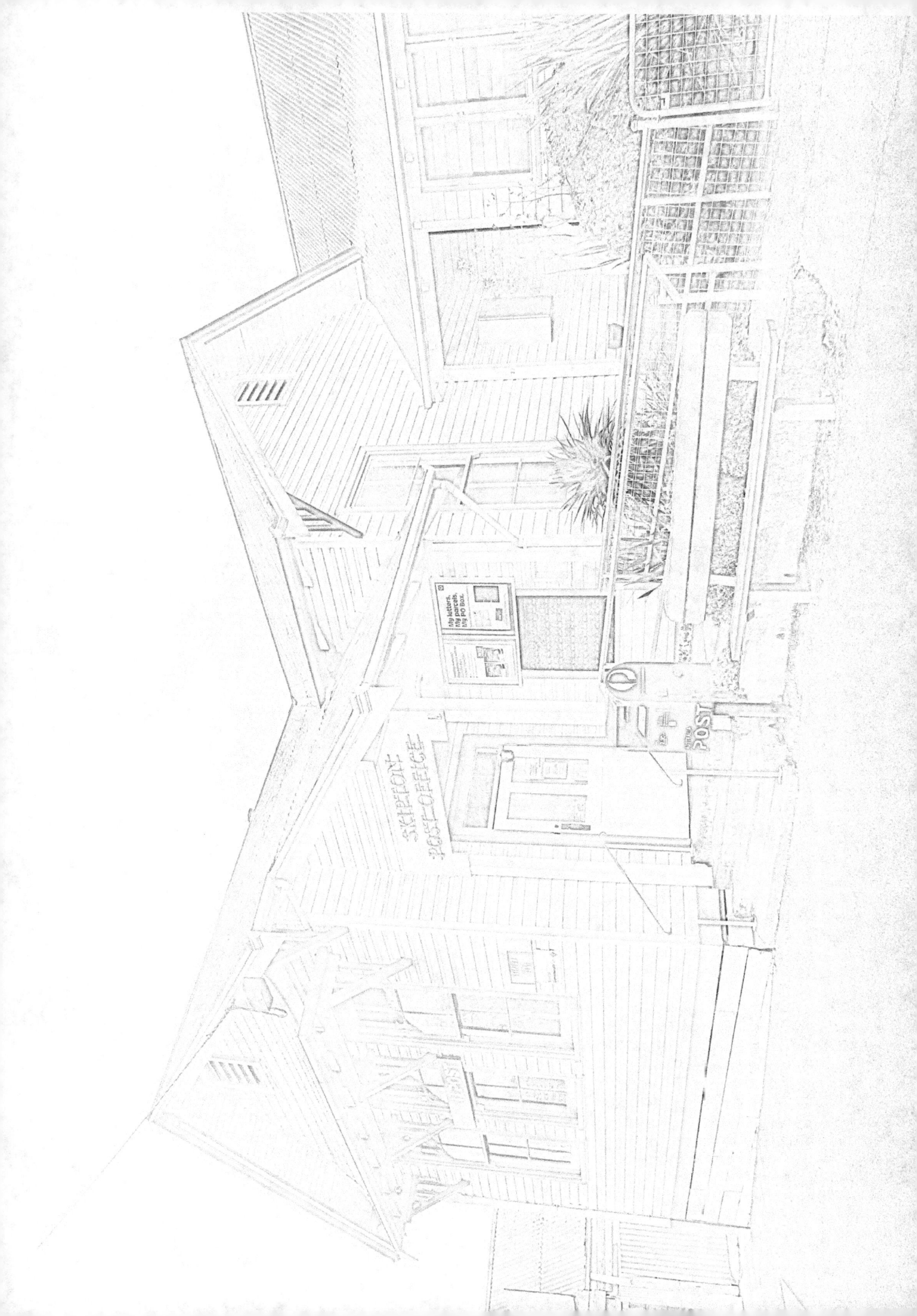

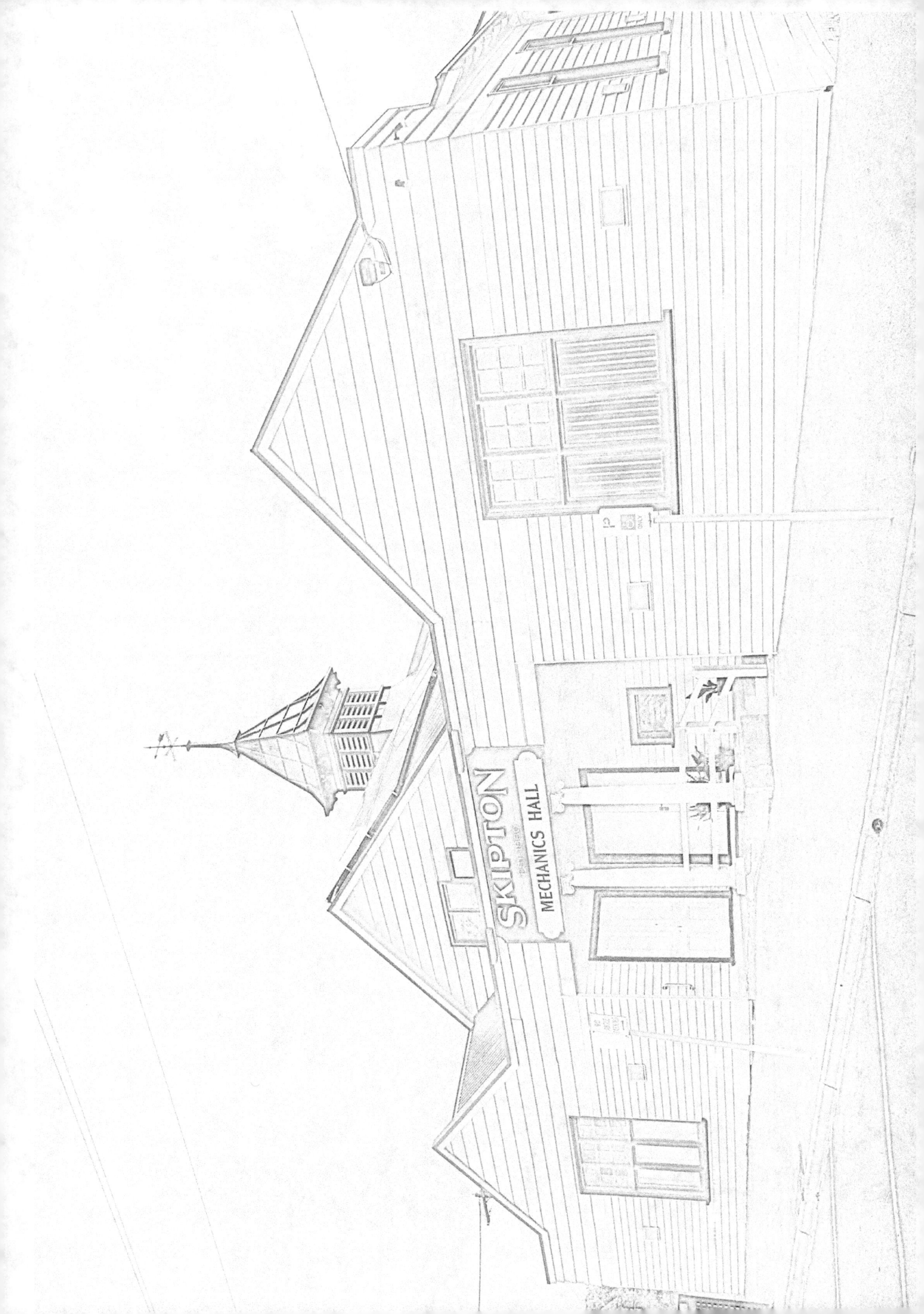

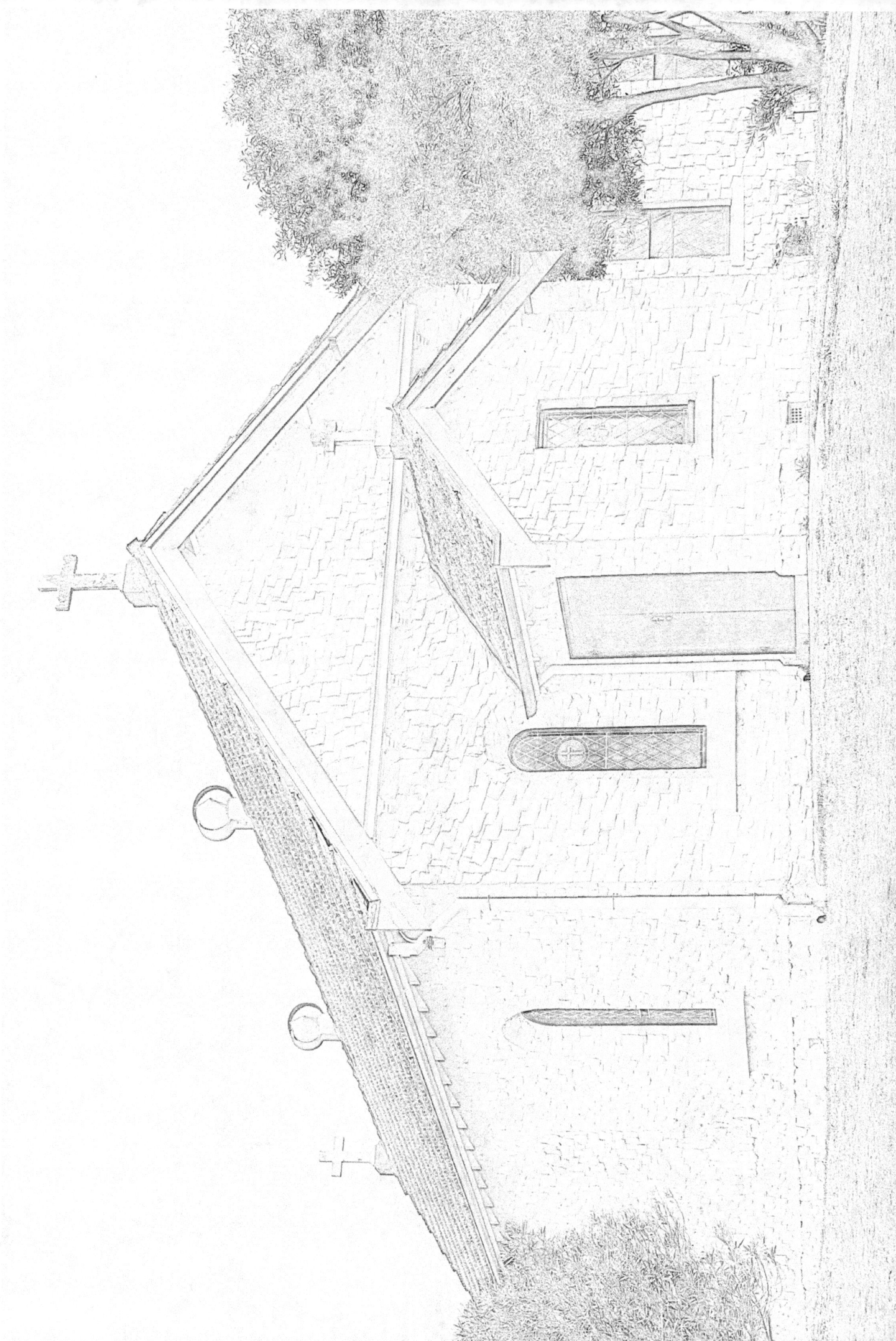

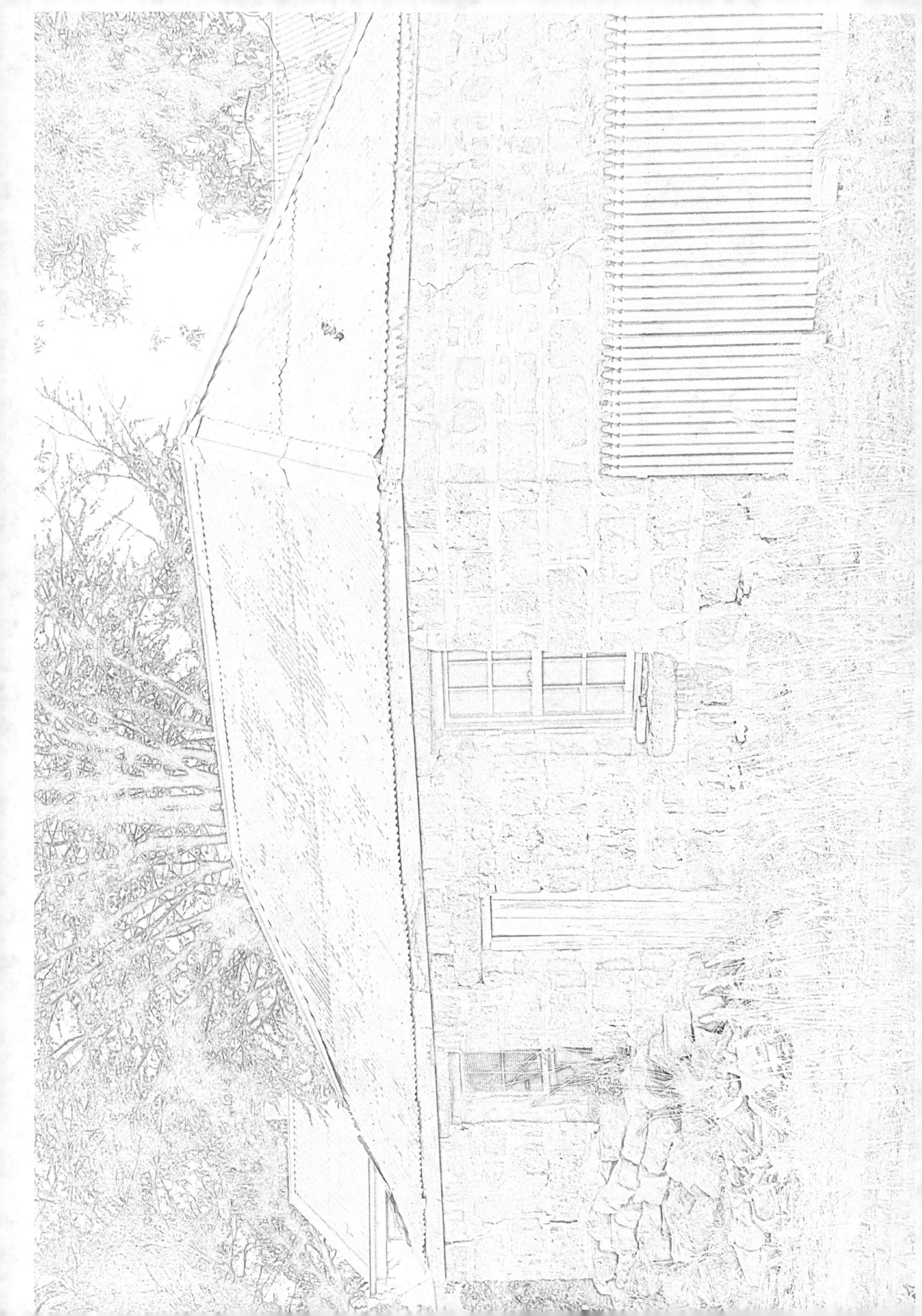

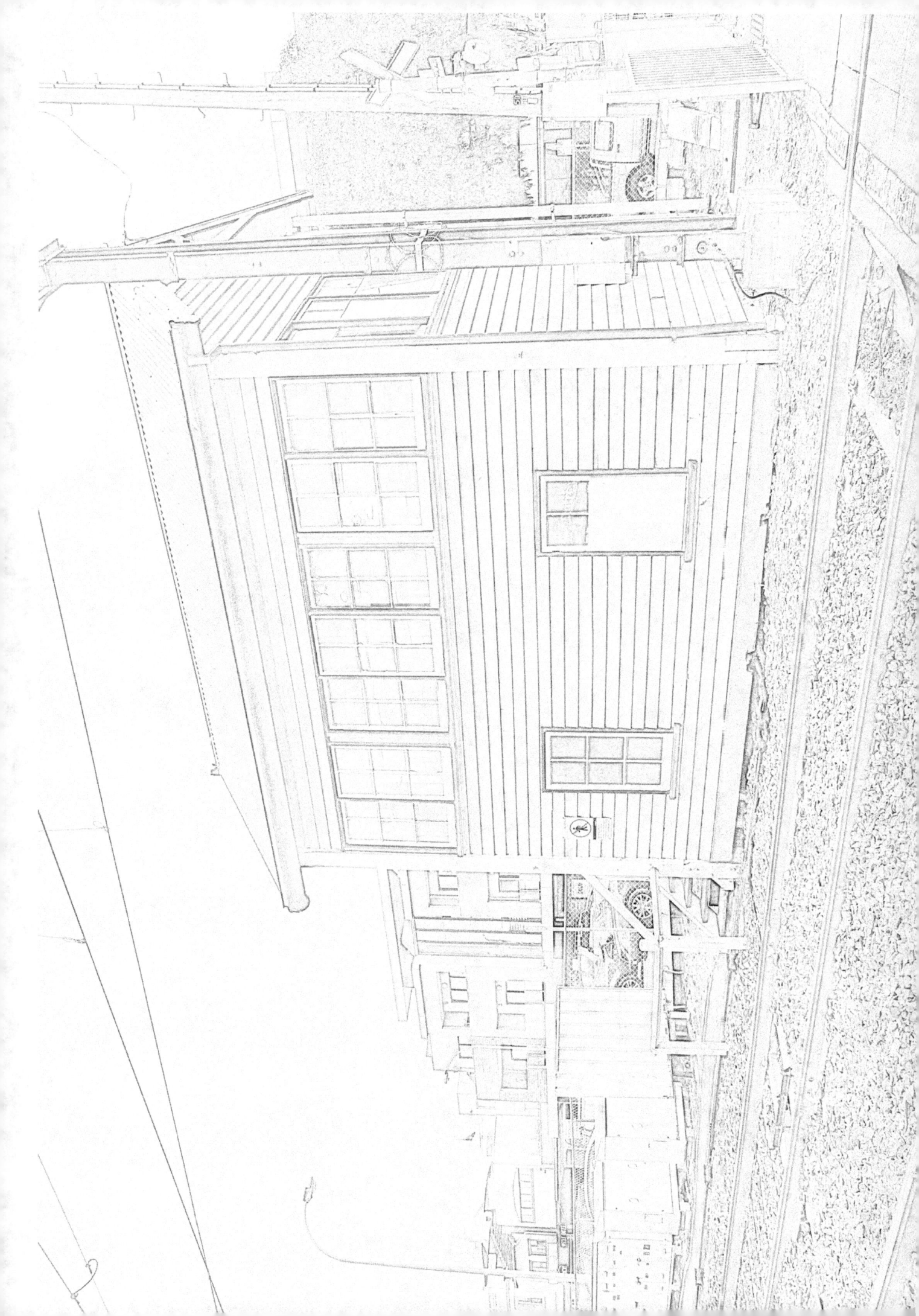

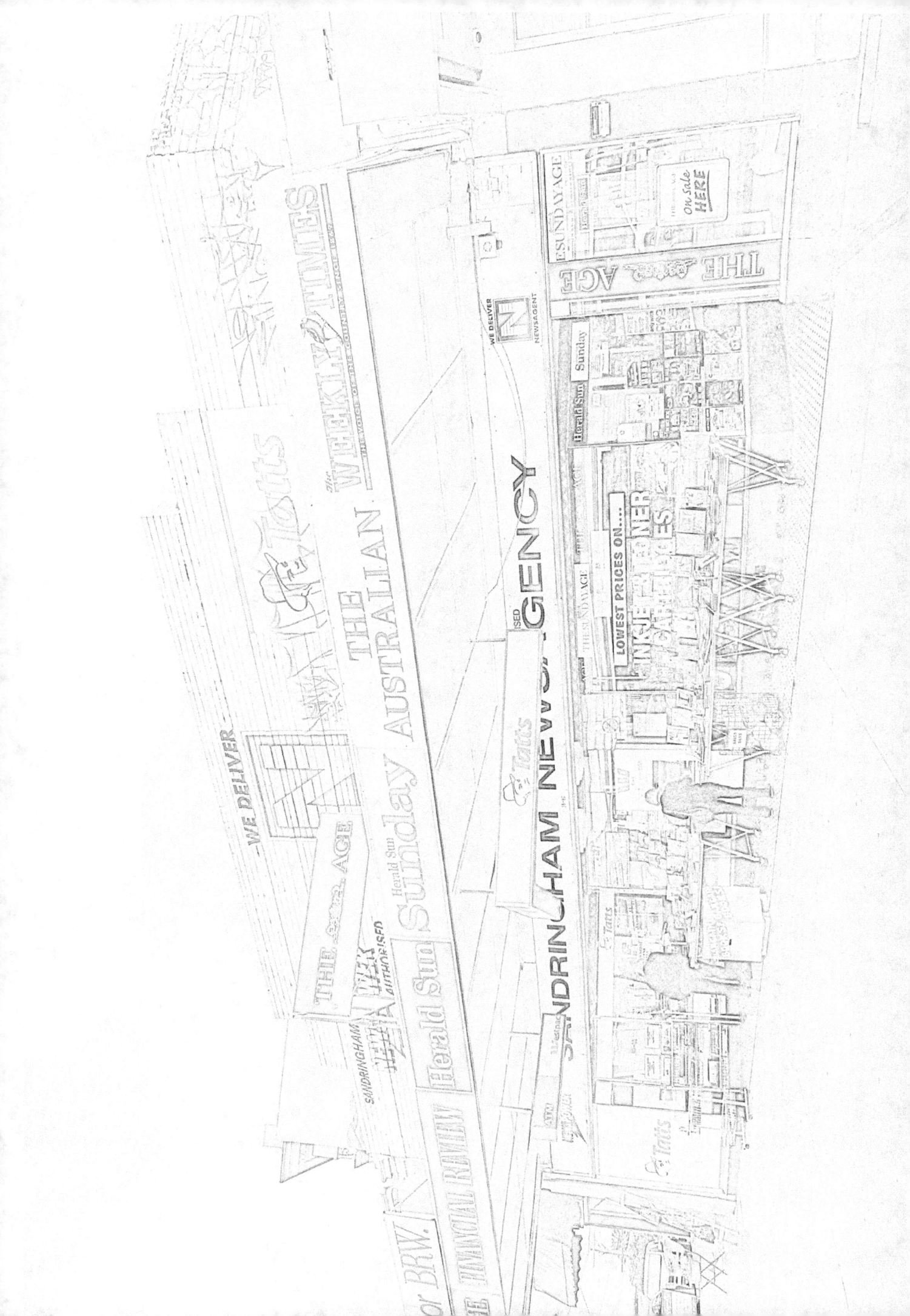

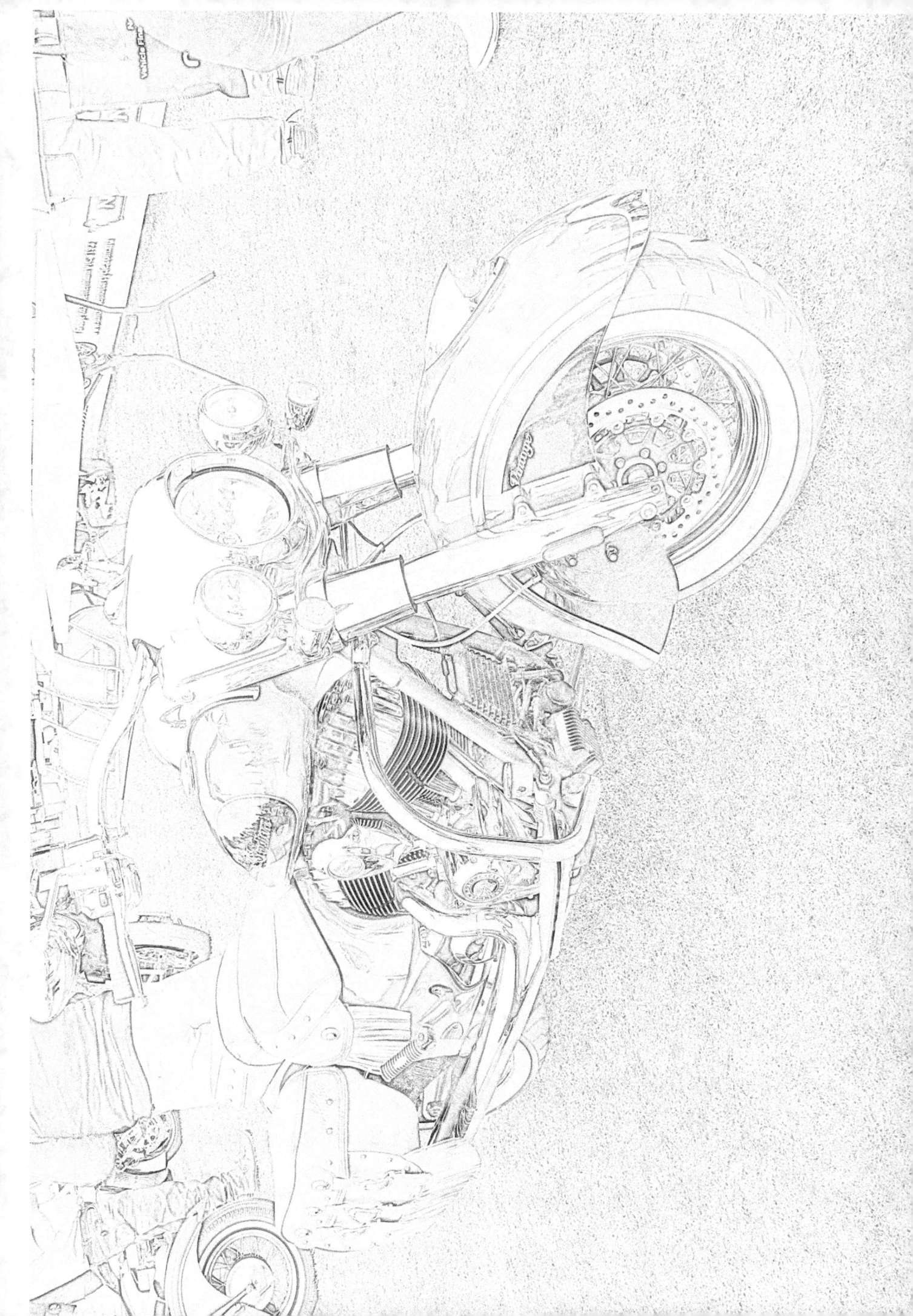

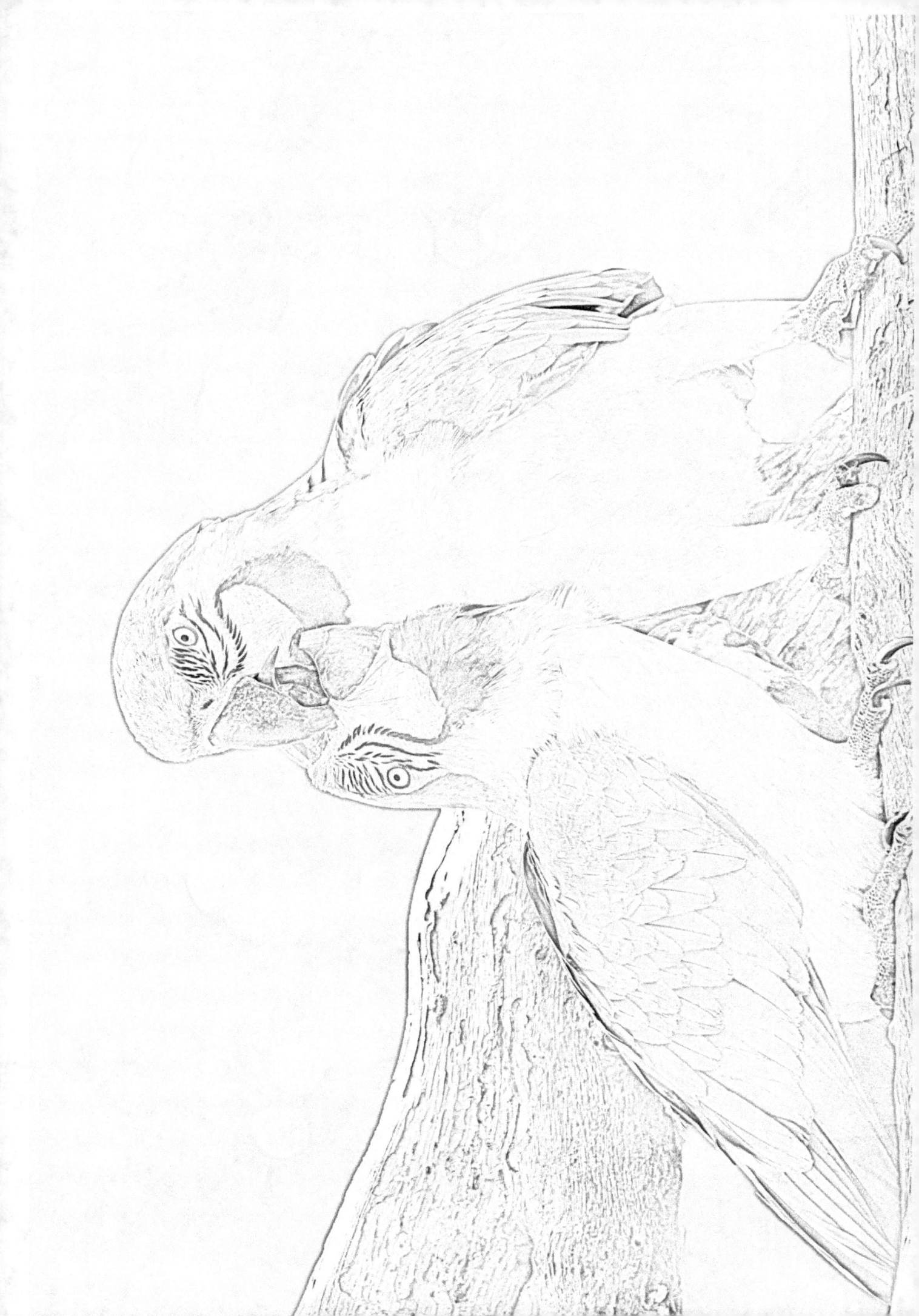

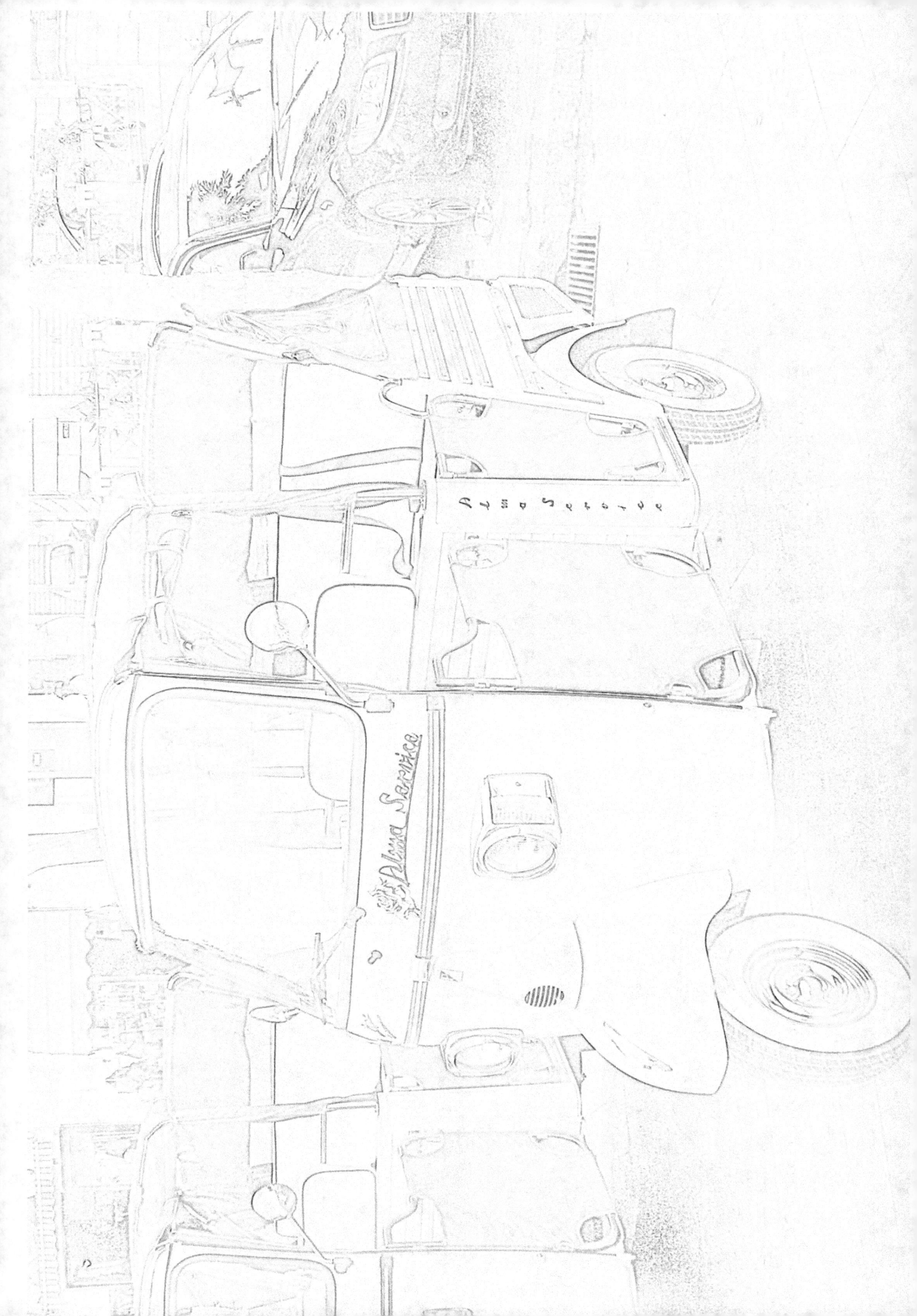

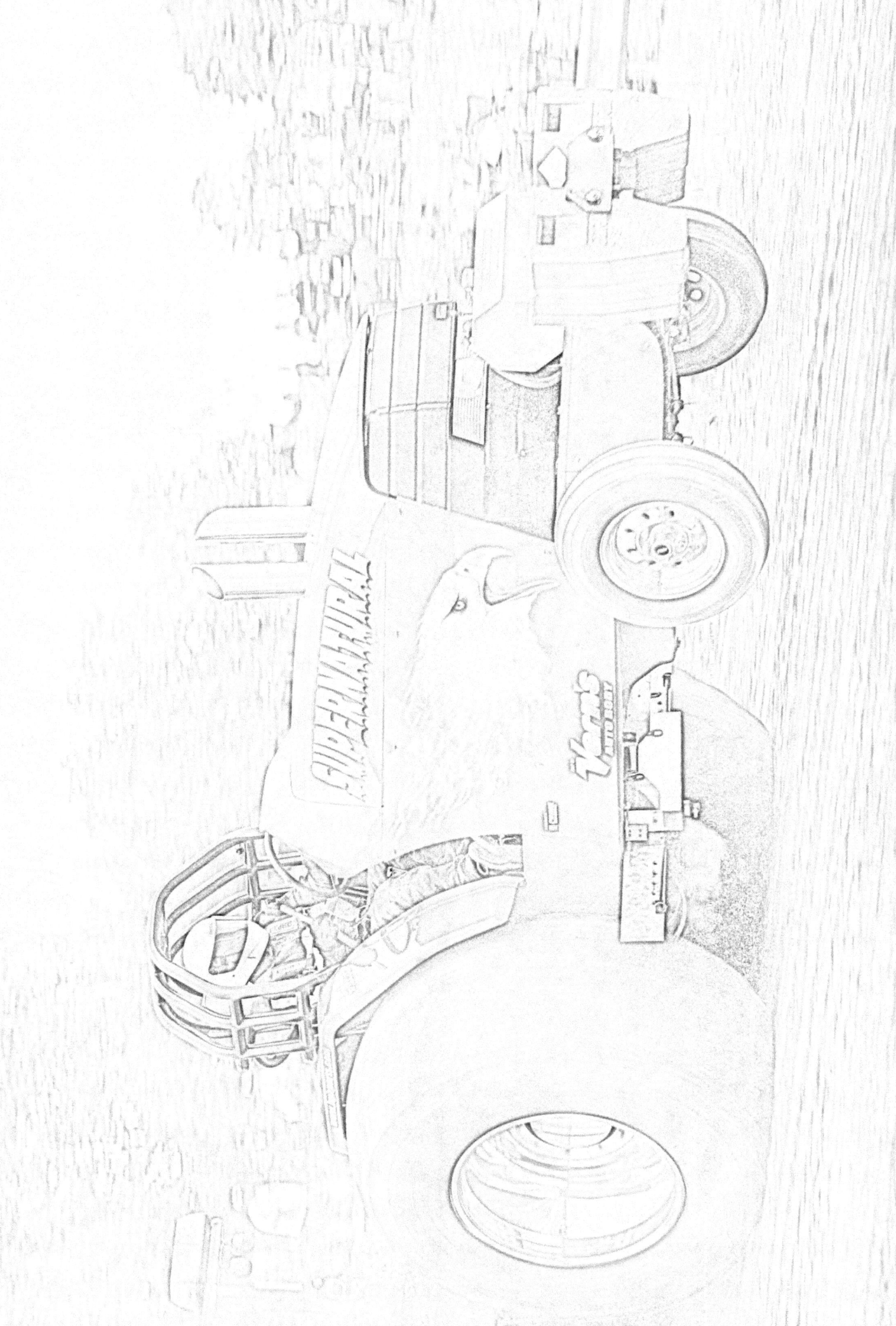

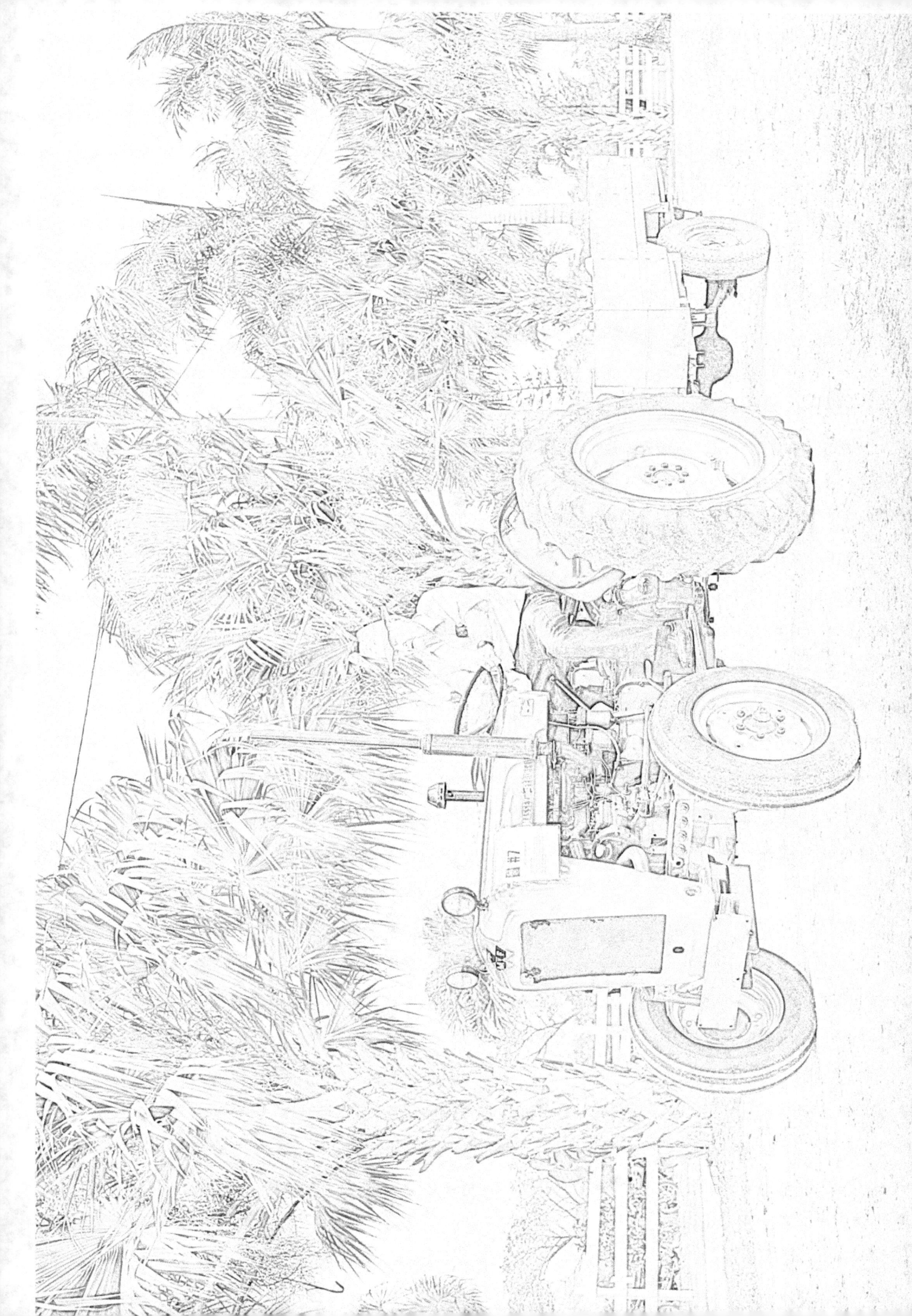

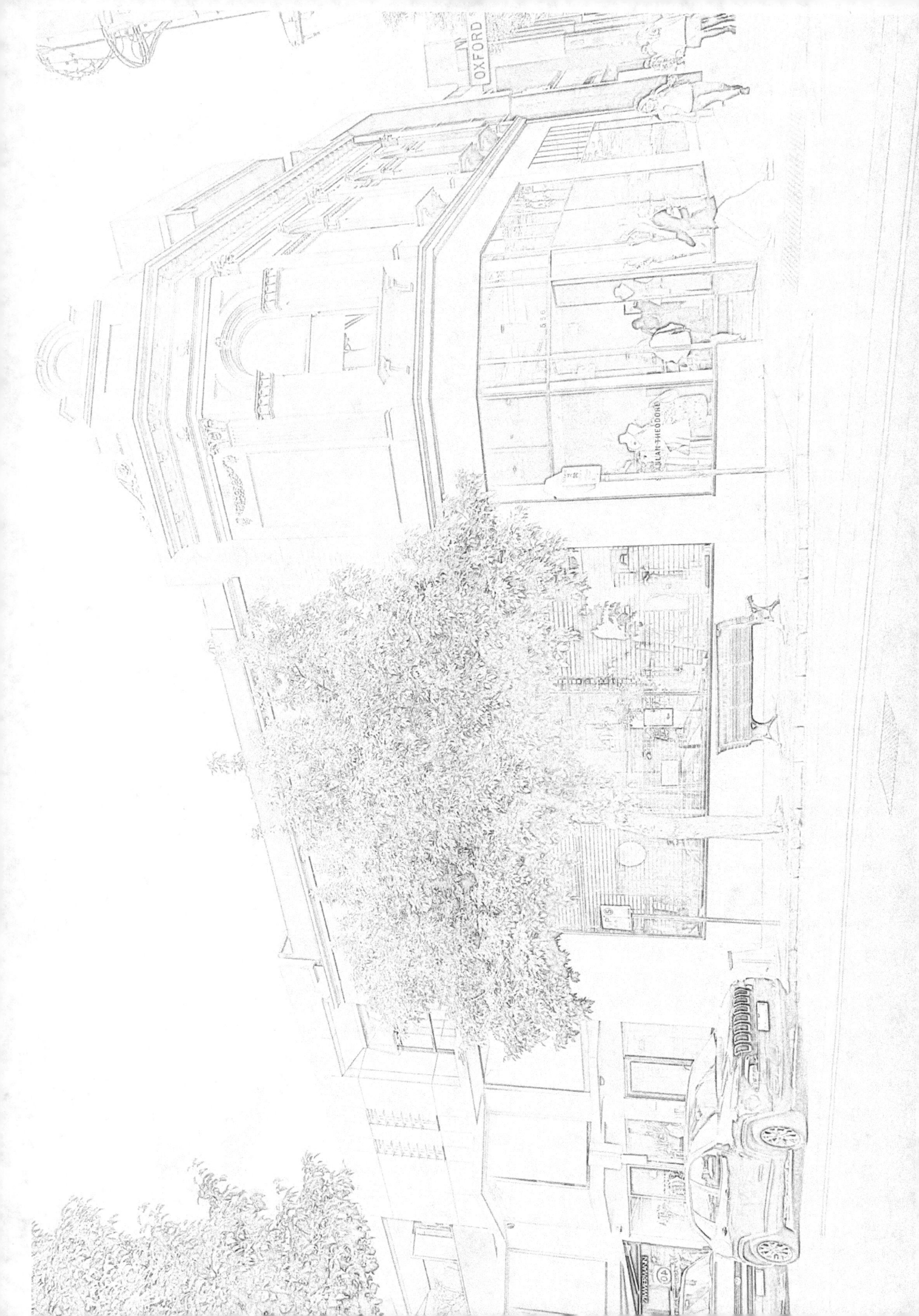

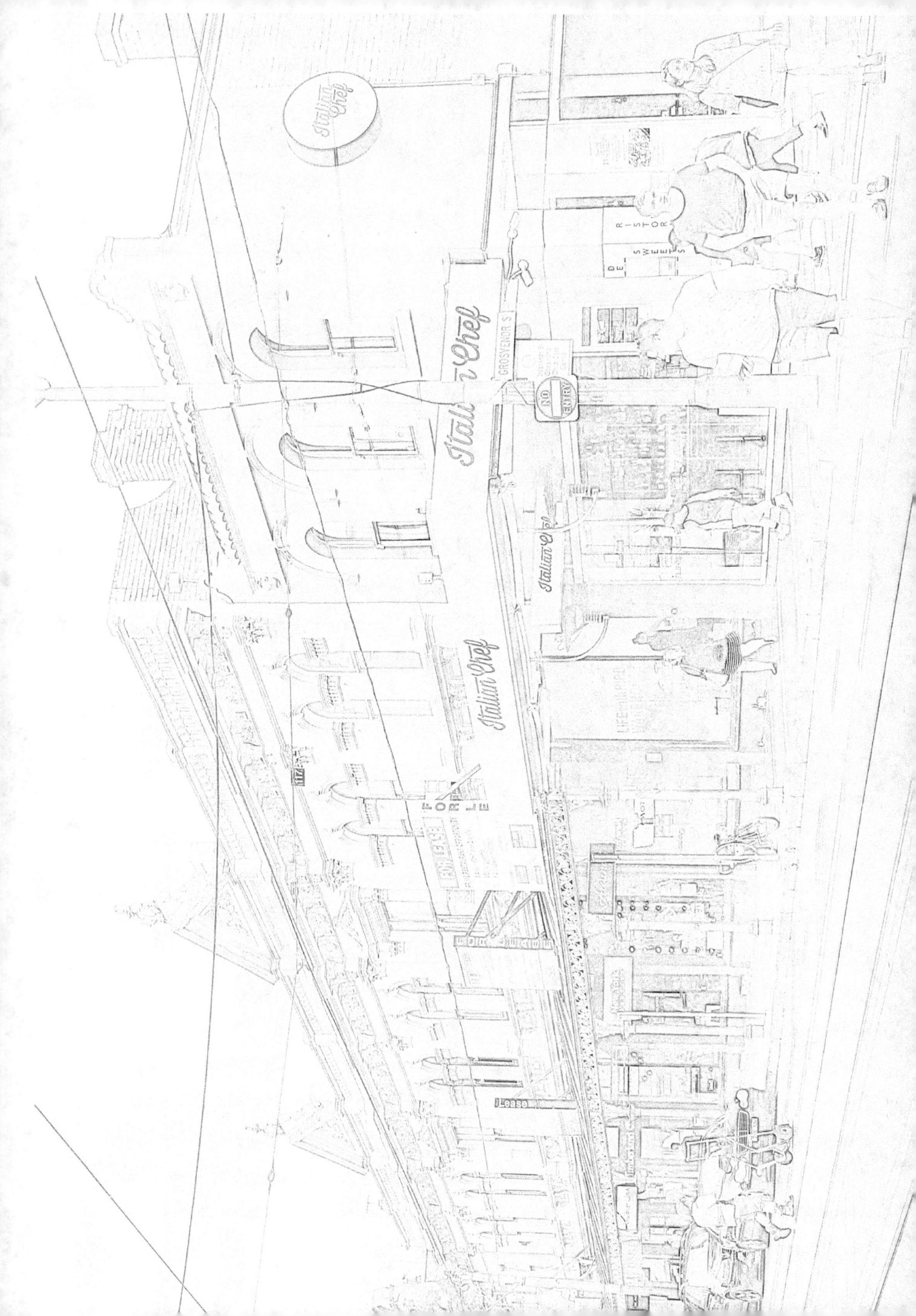

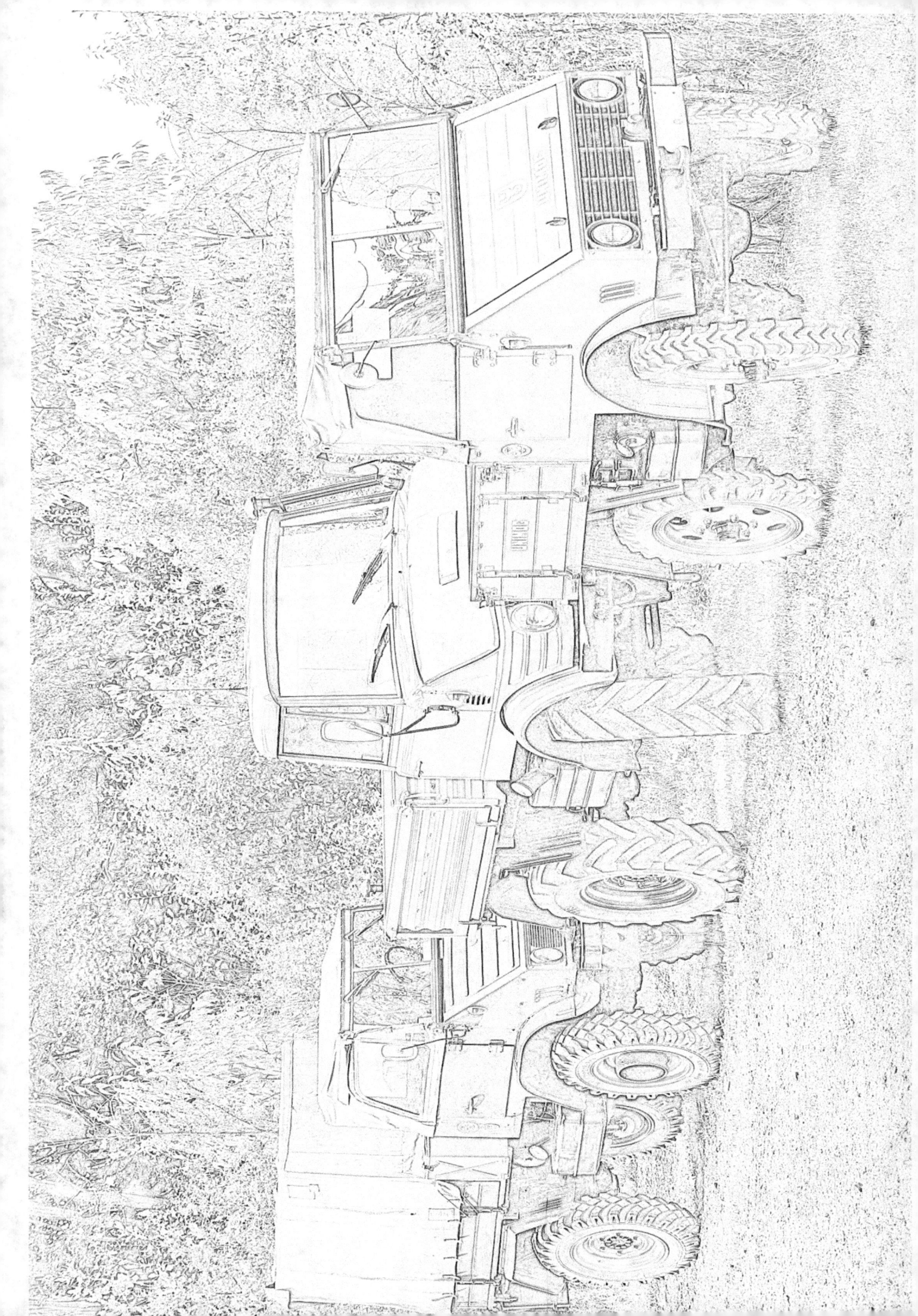